Developing Teachers' Theories of Teaching: A Touchstone Approach

Bevis G. Yaxley

 The Falmer Press

(A member of the Taylor & Francis Group)

London · New York · Philadelphia

UK   The Falmer Press, 4 John St, London WC1N 2ET
USA   The Falmer Press, Taylor & Francis Inc., 1900 Frost Road, Suite 101, Bristol, PA 19007

© B.G. Yaxley 1991

First published 1991

**British Library Cataloguing in Publication Data
is available on request**

**Library of Congress Cataloging-in-Publication Data
is available on request**

Set in 10½/13pt Bembo
by Graphicraft Typesetters Ltd, Hong Kong

*Printed in Great Britain by Burgess Science Press, Basingstoke
on paper which has a specified pH value on final paper
manufacture of not less than 7.5 and is therefore 'acid free'.*

Contents

Acknowledgments

This publication is the culmination of many years of working with teachers, from a very wide range of teaching areas and experience, in developing and conducting teacher development programs. These programs have encompassed many academic and professional perspectives. They have been concerned with the improvement of educational management, curriculum development and, most importantly, helping teachers come to understand and value the practical and theoretical insights of their challenging and demanding profession. This work owes much to the thoughtful dedication and inspiration of the many teachers I have been privileged to teach, and whose theories of teaching this study seeks to understand and enhance.

This book would not have been possible without the support and encouragement of Professor Phillip Hughes of the Centre for Education at the University of Tasmania; his wisdom of counsel and clarity of advice have been invaluable.

In addition, the completion of the study which this book reports would not have been possible without the unwavering love and kindness of my wife, Loris, to whom I wish to dedicate this small contribution to the enhancement of the profession which I have striven to serve.

Introduction

This is a book for teachers and those who work with teachers. It is about our search for effective teaching in times of increased demands for teacher accountability. It is about our attempts to describe what we believe to be effective teaching and to justify these descriptions publicly. It is, in particular, concerned with our striving to provide for those we teach the conditions for effective teaching and learning. It is concerned with teachers' knowledge and beliefs about effective teaching.

What do teachers know and believe about teaching? How do they come to this knowledge and belief, and how is this to be publicly justified? As teachers, we make claims to know about effective teaching and we espouse certain beliefs about it. Such sets of claims and beliefs are influential in our choosing what we do as teachers. They are our theories of effective teaching.

For these sets of claims and beliefs, our theories of teaching, two crucial questions must be asked. First, *how did we come to know what we claim to know about effective teaching*? Second, *how do we justify making these claims*? The answer to the first question will be a claim about how we learn or personally construct knowledge about teaching, a theory of learning or of personal constructs, whilst the second question must be answered in terms of how we justify the claim to have developed new knowledge about teaching. This latter answer may be described as a 'theory' of theory development.

If we are, as teachers, to study and develop our knowledge of effective teaching, we need ways of doing this. These methods must be such that they can be understood and conducted easily within schools and classrooms. They must be easily accessible to busy teachers. But if the new insights these procedures generate are to be accepted by both teachers and the wider educational community, they must also have a sound theoretical base which can be easily understood and appreciated by all concerned. Moreover, this theoretical basis must address the two key questions given above. The theoretical basis must contain both a theory of learning, or of personal constructs, and a theory of theory development.

Are there two such theories which would meet these requirements? Recent emphases in the study of teaching have shown a distinct movement away from seeing teaching as a technical matter, and effective teaching as being able to perform using a set of widely applicable skills, to viewing the teacher as a constructivist. From this perspective the teacher is constantly engaged in constructing new meanings, and effective teaching is seen in terms of the capacity to construct relevant meanings in the context in which the teacher is teaching and for those who are being taught. For the teacher as a constructivist, the question as to how teachers come to know about teaching becomes how teachers construct meaning for teaching in the context in which they are teaching. This question involves developing a theory of personal constructs.

Personal construct theory was initiated by George Kelly in 1955 with the publication of two volumes of his *Psychology of Personal Constructs*. Kelly's work has since been elaborated and extended, but still forms the theoretical basis for continuing studies of personal constructs. Because of the lucidity of Kelly's theory, and its underpinning assumptions, I have chosen it as the theory of personal constructs on which the exploration of teachers' theories of effective teaching can be based. This theory will be the answer to our first question.

But what is our basis for the claim that we know about effective teaching? This requires a theory of theory development. That is, it requires us to have a theoretical basis for judging whether the new theories or claims we have about effective teaching are 'better' than our previous theories or claims. In other words, has there been 'progress' in the development of knowledge and theories about effective teaching? Now the development of knowledge and beliefs about teaching tends to proceed not through sudden changes of direction but through the gradual modification, elaboration and extension of existing theories. We try to retain what is seen to be unhelpful from our present stock of knowledge about teaching, remove that which is shown, through practice, to be unhelpful and add those pieces which have the potential to be of assistance. We tend to concentrate on the helpful overlaps between competing theories and knowledge about effective teaching. We tend to look for commonalities and to reject aspects of competing theories which contrast radically. We tend to seek the overlaps between competing proposals for how we should teach effectively. We seek the touchstone between these competing theories. The answer to our second question, then, will be given in terms of a touchstone theory of theory development.

By bringing the two theoretical positions together we get a theoretical basis for the description, exploration, interpretation and review of teachers' knowledge, beliefs and theories about effective teaching. This basis allow us both to develop and to be able to justify procedures for the description, exploration, interpretation and review of these theories, knowledge and beliefs about effective teaching. This gives us a basis for the development of a clearer, more consistent and coherent, indeed more intelligible, discourse on effective teaching and places teachers and educators in a much better position to justify publicly, and be accountable for, the actions of teachers.

There are other advantages of this approach. Whilst the approach will be illustrated throughout this book using the problem of describing effective teaching as its central focus, it is not limited to this particular problem, important as it may be. Rather, it may be applied to any problem where the investigation and clarification of educational effectiveness are priorities. If, for example, a school wished to review the effectiveness of its decision-making, the conditions for making it effective could be examined using the strategies developed in this book. These strategies and their theoretical basis fit into the current emphasis on school effectiveness. In terms of developing an intelligible discourse about this effectiveness, this approach is of considerable importance to the school and teacher effectiveness movements. Throughout this book this approach is referred to as the 'touchstone approach to developing school and teacher effectiveness', in short, the 'touchstone approach'.

Using the touchstone approach to develop more intelligible descriptions and interpretations of the conditions for effectiveness is important in providing teachers with a basis for professional action and for justifying these actions, for being accountable on the basis of a publicly articulated and understood theoretical discourse on the effectiveness of schools and teachers. It follows that it is imperative that teachers become involved in the development and articulation of this professional discourse. Although there are, undoubtedly, many ways in which this involvement can be instigated and fostered, making it the primary focus of teacher development programs is a powerful way of ensuring that the development of this professional discourse gets the attention it deserves. At the heart of teacher development is the enhancement of the capacities of teachers to describe and publicly justify intelligibly the conditions for effective practice.

To illustrate the touchstone approach, this book describes the

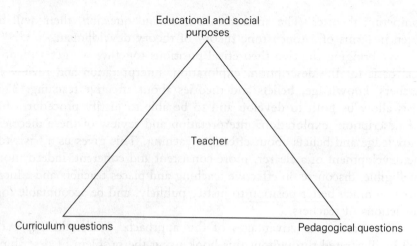

Figure 1. *Interactions of Elements of Schooling*

development and application of this approach to a teacher development program for a group of experienced and senior teachers. Before the theoretical and procedural basis for the touchstone approach is discussed, it will be helpful to consider the context of schools and teaching today. Schools, and those who work in them, are concerned with achieving educational and social purposes. The formal attempts to reach these purposes are through the teaching of a curriculum. These purposes are both social and educational and are derived from both the needs and interests of students and society, and from our notions of educating. Once determined, these purposes are a basis for determining the curriculum to be followed. The content of the curriculum, in terms of knowledge, skills and attitudes, should provide for these needs and interests and, at the same time, make possible the educating of each student. It is the task of the school, and particularly of its teachers, to ensure that student learning opportunities are provided through this curriculum and to enable the purposes to be met.

This may sound clear and systematic and linear, but is this how it really is? Schools are dynamic; they are characterized by interaction, by shifting patterns of interaction and by shifting purposes. There is a dynamic and evolving interaction between the purposes a school seeks to achieve, the curriculum it wishes students to experience and the approaches to teaching used. The school has to deal with three sets of crucial questions relating to (i) educational and social purposes; (ii) the curriculum; and (iii) pedagogy. Our answers to any of these questions may affect our answers to all other questions. The process may be depicted as in Figure 1.

In the figure the teacher is placed at the centre of gravity of the triangle, since the dynamic interplay of questions and answers impinges directly on the teacher. It is the teacher who has the critical task of balancing competing demands from purposes, curriculum and teaching resources and approaches. As teaching approaches change, so do curriculum content and educational and social purposes.

All of our purposes are, in the end, expressions of meaning, values and beliefs about our experience of the world. In particular, educational purposes express meanings, values and beliefs about: (i) the nature of humanity, or what it is to be a person, our ideas of personhood; (ii) the nature of the society in which we live; and (iii) the knowledge which is most worthwhile for us to know, our view of the content of the curriculum.

In the past these meanings, beliefs and values have been seen in terms of reflecting the *present* views of personhood, society and of the curriculum. Given our commitment to the recognition and accommodation of change, the sets of meanings, beliefs and values which now constitute our theories of educating are more likely to reflect views of a future, an educational vision. The meanings, beliefs and values are future-forming, rather than past-conserving. Increasingly, the nature of society, humanity and what we need to know and be able to do is considered in terms of visions of possible futures. Moreover, these visions are those of a post-industrial society, including emphases on science and technology, economic rationality, devolving responsibility, and strengthening commitments to enact fully the principles of a political democracy.

Within this context schools, and by implication teaching, are coming under increasing public scrutiny and associated demands for public accountability. Increasingly, teachers will be at the centre of these demands. Their capacities to articulate in publicly intelligible ways what they are doing and why they are doing it will be the focus of public attention and criticism. Being clear about what counts as effective teaching, and how we can improve the quality of our teaching are now matters of vital concern for all of us.

In the discussion of teaching, there is a distinction which has far-reaching consequences for the way we conduct such discussions: teaching can be seen in terms of either activities or accomplishments, as tasks or achievements. We must be careful to distinguish those activities which we denote as teaching from the accomplishment which these activities may have helped achieve. The activities of teaching the division of fractions must be distinguished from the accomplishment of having completed a set of exercises involving the division of fractions. Teaching is activity as distinct from accomplishment.

A further distinction may also be necessary: between the activities and accomplishments of teaching and the conditions necessary for the activities of teaching to lead to these accomplishments. We distinguish: (i) the activities which constitute and define teaching (*teaching*); (ii) the accomplishments of the students resulting from these activities (*outcomes*); and (iii) the conditions which must apply for these activities of teaching to enable their accomplishment (*conditions*). These distinctions are important, since we must be clear as to what constitutes and defines teaching. *Teaching is defined in terms of its constituent activities.*

Teaching as a set of activities is a central concept of educating. This is supported by a philosophical tradition for the study of teaching, which has its origins with Plato, was further enlightened by Aristotle, and has its modern-day contributors in scholars such as Israel Scheffler, Paul Hirst, Maxine Green and Fenstermacher. It is further supported by an empirical tradition for the study of teaching to which Gage, Berliner and Rosenshine are three of the many important contributors. From both traditions, teaching, and hence its study and the need to understand it, is crucial to educating. Recent approaches to the study of teaching have stressed the importance of practitioner knowledge of teaching and the need for teachers to reflect critically on this knowledge. From such study a strong interest has developed in exploring teachers' beliefs about teaching and learning and the ways these may shape practice.

The position put forward here has been influenced by both traditions. Indeed, it reflects recent concerns to bring these traditions into agreement and mutual support. Central to the view espoused here is the notion that teaching is *intentional*. All teaching activities carry with them purposes or intentions. These purposes, and their underlying beliefs, are seen as critical determinants for teacher action, as are the purposes of students in responding to this action.

Underlying this notion is the presumption that human beings act in accord with the beliefs and values they hold about the meaning of their experiences of the world. The intentionalist view of teaching places beliefs, value and meaning at centre-stage. Teaching is about intentional action which leads to changes in belief, value and meaning. Teaching, therefore, is concerned with confirming, changing, reviewing, testing, describing, etc. beliefs, values and meanings.

Teaching is also an intellectual activity. It involves thinking, feeling and valuing. That is, the interaction between the teacher and students, or indeed between student and students, which we call teaching is a *series of intellectual acts*. These include describing, explaining, reviewing, criticizing, hypothesizing and analyzing. All of these activities are purpose-driven. *Teaching is engagement in an intentional set of intellectual acts.* It is an intentional, intellectual matter.

Such acts attend to both the cognitive and the affective. Teaching as engagement is concerned with thinking about what we know, what we are able to do, our values, our beliefs and the meanings we attribute to experience. Teaching is concerned with the cognitive and the moral. The intellectual acts which constitute an engagement in teaching are purposeful and are enacted in relation to a particular content. To engage in teaching is to apply a range of intellectual acts to some subject matter; and this will assist the changes of someone's (the student's) beliefs, values and meanings. Teaching involves teaching *something* to someone else.

The 'something' is, of course, the curriculum. At this point, therefore, it is appropriate to comment on current notions of curriculum development and how these might relate to evolving views of teaching and educating. These comments must be brief and hence may suffer from being oversimplified and truncated. Nevertheless, it is suggested that whereas until recent times the content of our teaching was seen as providing students with the answers to questions that someone else had decided were important, emerging trends in curriculum development suggest that the curriculum is guided not by sets of answers, but by sets of questions. That is, we are now concerned with helping students pose questions appropriate to their interests and needs and assisting them to explore possible answers to these questions. This is an important shift, reflecting a fundamental change in our view of knowledge from certainty to conjectural, or problematic, and in our teaching from providing for the receipt of pre-packaged answers to facilitating the posing and exploration of important questions. The coherence of our educational purposes, curricula and teaching is now being thought of in terms of values, beliefs and meaning which underpin a view of the student as a self-directed and culturally reflective learner within an evolving political democracy which emphasizes self-determination and individuality, but which, at the same time, stresses entrepreneurship within a framework of collegial and social responsibility. Within this framework, there has been a major shift in our views of the nature of society, of personhood, and of knowledge.

Given this context, briefly stated, it becomes clear that the assumed notion of personhood means that teachers, and hence teaching, require a commitment to self-directed learning, to self-criticism, evaluation and development. But this evaluation and development should have as their focus teaching, and specifically teaching as engagement within those intentional, intellectual acts which characterize teaching. This is not to say that we should not also pay attention to teachers' capacities to provide the conditions necessary for this teaching to take place — to secure effective management of learning, in particular. Nor is it to diminish in any way the importance of considering the effectiveness of teaching in terms of what the students learn — the accomplishment of teaching. Rather, it is to reaffirm that without effective engagement in intellectual interaction, whether this be by direct engagement with the teacher or indirectly through learning experiences, the capacities of students to become self-directed learners, to become educated, will not be enhanced.

From this point of view, it is suggested that teaching someone something involves helping that person explore possible answers to the questions that they should ask, given their intellectual predicament in relation to their development as persons, their place within and potential contribution to society, and the conjectural, problematic and evolving nature of knowing and knowledge. It is stressed that the intellectual predicament of the student is both cognitive and affective. It involves what the student should learn and the meanings, beliefs and values they need to explore. How do we assess and monitor intellectual predicament?

In particular, engagement in the activities of teaching, and therefore of learning, requires a cognitive and moral commitment on the part of both teacher and taught, on the part of all participants in the engagement. Teaching is a cognitive/moral activity. It involves meanings, beliefs and values about the moral, and hence social, conduct of our lives. Important-ly, the forms of engagement in teaching, whether they be lectures, group work, reporting, storying and so on, must be underpinned by meanings, beliefs and values which are acceptable within today's culture. This would include those meanings, beliefs and values which it is acceptable to challenge and criticize. Thus engagement in teaching occurs within cultural norms and beliefs. This is, perhaps, typified by the current em-phases on cooperative learning, which accords with a movement towards collegial responsibility. Similarly, problem-solving as a form of engage-ment for teaching is increasingly valued.

accepted norms and values, there will be corresponding changes both in what counts as acceptable accomplishments resulting from teaching, and in the conditions required for reaching these accomplishments; that is, for effective teaching. Each form of engagement is characterized by different sets of intellectual acts, and different mixes of these acts. The lecture as a form of engagement in teaching relies heavily on describing and explain-ing, and the capacities of students to become engaged, cognitive-ly and morally committed, within these activities. Working in groups, however, involves sharing, reviewing, discussing and so on. For each form of engagement in teaching there will be, likewise, different accomp-lishments and conditions. In particular, the form of engagement and its constituent intellectual acts affect the manner in which students come to know, contribute meaning and acquire values and beliefs. If I learn about teaching through being thoroughly engrossed in the film *The Dead Poet's Society*, I know, understand, feel, believe about and value teaching in a different way from learning about it through listening intently to a lecture on teaching strategies.

We are now teaching through forms of engagement that help the student come to know, understand, believe and value in ways which relate to visions of future, to which we subscribe, which may be thrust upon us, or are considered as possible futures. *The crucial debate concerns the sensitive interrelationships between educational vision and the purposes entailed, the content of the curriculum appropriate to these purposes and the forms of engagement in teaching essential to these purposes and curriculum*. At the heart of the current educational debate we must place teaching – teaching as forms of engagement in intellectual acts, those intellectual acts which cohere with our visions of evolving personhood, society and the meanings, values and beliefs which underpin them. This is the educational agenda of the future. Crucial to this agenda is the question as to how teachers make decisions about the actions they will take in teaching.

Teachers claim various degrees of expertise in teaching. These claims are both claims to know about effective teaching and beliefs about effective teaching. As a teacher, I may claim to know that, for example, effective teaching can only take place when all learning activities are predetermined by the teacher, or that children can learn the skills of cooperating only by studying in groups with other children. Such knowledge claims may be justified by the teacher on the grounds of their experience as teachers. Other claims about effective teaching may not be easily justified, even on the grounds that it works in practice. When questioned about such claims, teachers may admit that they do not know that these actions will always lead to effective teaching but believe it to be the case. As a teacher, I believe that my feelings towards those whom I teach, whether I feel positively or not, will influence the effectiveness of my teaching of them. This claim will be difficult to justify as a knowledge claim, but it may remain as a strongly held belief.

Teacher actions are usually justified in terms of knowledge claims and beliefs about teaching. These knowledge claims and beliefs about effective teaching will be referred to here as teachers' theories of effective teaching; they are the focus of this book. As teachers, we are not always aware of our theories of teaching. Indeed, it is often only when we are challenged to justify our actions as teachers that we begin to articulate and become aware of these theories. Again, we will at times be quite explicit about them; at other times and in the absence of demands to account publicly for our actions, these theories remain implicit. Implicit theories of teaching will include our underlying beliefs, values and presuppositions about effective teaching. As the demands for public evaluation of teaching increase, so will the necessity for teachers, and those who manage education, to be able to describe and justify the actions of teachers in publicly intelligible and practically plausible ways. To do so, teachers may have to move beyond the statement and justification of their immediately explicit theories of teaching to bring into consciousness, to describe, review and publicly justify their implicit theories as well.

This book describes, using actual examples, how exploration and critical review of both the explicit and implicit theories of teachers may be undertaken, and gives a theoretical justification for these procedures. The theories which are examined refer to the conditions for effective teaching of a particular focus class selected by each teacher as described by the teacher of that class. This exploration was conducted within the context of the planning, conduct and evaluation of a teacher development program in which the participants were experienced, senior teachers. The aim of this program was to assist the participants to explore and review critically their explicit and implicit theories of effective teaching for their focus class, and, as a result of this review, to enhance the intelligibility of their descriptions of the conditions for effective teaching for this class. In this way, the professional conversations on effective teaching of this group of teachers would become more intelligible to these teachers and, in the longer term, to the educational public.

Chapter 1

Planning for the Teacher Development Program

This book is based on a case study of a teacher development program. For the teachers taking part, the focus of this program was the description of effective teaching and learning. The planning, conduct and evaluation of the effectiveness of the teacher development program involved:

  i the planning and conduct of program;

  ii developing a reading content for the program;

  iii monitoring and assessing changes in the intelligibility of the teachers' descriptions of effective teaching and learning;

  iv evaluating the effectiveness of the program in meeting its purposes for the teachers.

The Problem: Describing Effective Teaching and Learning

We are concerned with the theories of effective teaching and learning held by individual teachers participating in the teacher development program. For each teacher, these theories will refer to a focus class previously selected by that teacher, and will be stated as descriptions of effective teaching and learning for that class.

Teachers working in schools share many problems. These include problems of curriculum content and assessment procedures, and problems relating to the organization of teaching and learning. Given the interdependence of curriculum, organization and teacher development, attempts to bring about changes in the curriculum, organization or teaching of a school must raise questions related to effective teaching and learning. That is, the problem of describing effective teaching and learning is a problem common to all teachers in a school, and shared by them in any search for solutions to problems in teaching, curriculum and school organization. This suggests that the teacher development program must emphasize the sharing among participating teachers of the problems, and their possible solutions, perceived by these teachers as associated with describing effective teaching and learning.

The descriptions of effective teaching and learning given by teachers will vary. These varying descriptions may be taken to indicate personal, different theories of effective teaching and learning. That is, each teacher is stating a different set of knowledge claims or beliefs, personal theories, relating to effective teaching and learning. These theories, or sets of knowledge claims or beliefs, provide various solutions to the problem of describing effective teaching and learning. Thus these theories are said to be competing. The touchstone approach to theory development, when applied to the problem of describing effective teaching and learning, is concerned with finding a coherent resolution of competing theories of effective teaching and learning. It does so by focusing on the agreements and disagreements between such theories.

Which theories are in competition with one another is a function of both the problem being considered and the general fabric of the teacher's knowledge and beliefs about effective teaching and learning. The extent to which this general fabric of knowledge is shared among teachers, or is idiosyncratic, will determine the degree to which various theories of effective teaching and learning will be in competition.

For these reasons the emphasis in the teacher development program is on:

    i   the shared problem of describing effective teaching and learning;
    ii sharing theories which propose alternative solutions to this problem;
    iii identifying the agreements and disagreements among these competing theories;
    iv resolving these by finding the solution which is most coherent with the knowledge of, and beliefs about, effective teaching and learning;

These emphases suggest:

    i   sharing among the teachers in the program;
    ii additional theoretical input to the program, and the sharing of this and its implications for effective teaching and learning, among the teachers;
    iii sharing and negotiation among teachers to identify the agree-

ments and disagreements between their personal theories of effective teaching;

iv each teacher attempting to resolve these agreements and disagreements by finding the solution, which is most coherent with their current knowledge of, and beliefs about, effective teaching and learning.

Applying the Touchstone Approach

Different teachers usually have different personal theories of effective teaching. As these theories are concerned with solving the same problem, namely the conditions for effective teaching, they are called competing theories. The touchstone for these theories consists of the overlap between them. Thus the touchstone could include common claims and beliefs about effective teaching.

In applying the touchstone approach, the first task is to find such overlaps. This touchstone, or overlap, between competing theories of teaching can never be foundational. It is not possible to find one theory of teaching from which all other theories may be derived. Rather, the touchstone is that shifting and changing body of shared claims and beliefs about effective teaching common to the various competing theories of teaching. The touchstone is always relative to these competing theories as they stand at any particular time. The touchstone in one context may not be the same in another. The touchstone for a given set of competing educational theories may, for example, be different for primary education and secondary education.

The touchstone approach focuses on the agreements and disagreements between competing theories. It assumes open competition between those theories conducted in an open-minded way (Walker and Evers, 1983). Theories compete with one another when they propose alternative solutions to common problems. Touchstone theory development is directed towards the solution of shared problems.

For the touchstone approach, the search for knowledge is a problem-solving process. Knowledge grows through the solution of shared problems. But how is it known what constitutes a problem, and which problems are more important? Problems, and their relative importance to other problems, will be identified by applying our current whole sets of knowledge claims and beliefs, or theories, to the present situation. In this sense touchstone theory assumes a holistic epistemology, and is self-referential. As such, the justification of a theory of teaching depends upon the coherence of the theory with the general fabric of knowledge and beliefs about teaching in relation to the particular problem of describing effective teaching, and clashes between competing theories are resolved by adopting the most coherent solution (theory). For the touchstone approach the critical notion is that of 'coherence'.

Developing Coherent Theories of Teaching and Learning

To explore the notion of coherence, consider a set of statements made in an axiomatic system, such as Euclidean geometry. Such a set of statements may, for example, form the proof of a theorem or proposition in Euclidean geometry. Thus we may seek to prove that the angles at the base of an isosceles triangle are equal. In this case the set of statements forming the proof will provide an understanding of the proposal being proved. This understanding may be considered in two senses: first, that the understanding provided by the set of statements is coherent; and second, that it is a plausible.

The set of statements constituting a proof in Euclidean geometry is coherent in two ways. In the first place, the set of statements should be logically consistent. That is, they must be free from any contradictions. The proof that the base angles of the isoceles traingle are equal does not contain statements which are mutually contradictory. Second, the statements within the proof must be linked together to form an interrelated pattern. This is the case when each statement refers to, or implies, at least one other statement so that all the statements are linked together into one interconnected network. This interconnected network is the proof of the theorem, for example. Thus a network of co-referencing can be established for the set of statements. This property of the set of statements will be referred to as connectedness. For a set of statements in Euclidean geometry, or any other axiomatic system, the coherency of these statements can be considered in terms of their logical consistency and connectedness.

Similar arguments may be applied to a set of statements describing effective teaching and learning. Whilst this set of statements does not form a logically deductive network, as is the case for the proof of a theorem in Euclidean geometry, its coherence can be considered in terms of its connectedness and consistency.

In an intelligible description of effective teaching and learning, a contributing factor to the intelligibility is the coherence of the description. Does the description fit together? Is it free of contradictory statements? Are the statements consistent in meanings, beliefs and values? Are the statements interconnected through, for example, co-referencing? Each description is composed of semantic units. In most cases these are sentences; in this case, they are statements describing effective teaching and learning. A requirement for the description to be coherent is that each semantic unit refers to another semantic unit, and so on. That is, the various sentences are linked, through co-referencing for example, to form a coherent description. A primary contributing factor for the coherence of descriptions is the co-referencing of the sentences of this description.

Each sentence, or semantic unit, within a description refers to its object, or objects. The sentence also ascribes to its object(s) certain properties, as well as relations with other objects. Thus in a description of effective teaching and learning, the student will be the object of many of the sentences used. Moreover, these sentences will ascribe properties such as intelligence and curiosity to the student, and will indicate, for instance, a relationship between student curiosity and cognitive achievement. The coherence of such a description will be indicated, also, by the extent to which the properties and relations ascribed are consistent with one another, and, in particular, free from contradictions. Consistency of properties and relations is a contributing factor to the coherence of the description.

In the teacher development program, the evidence relating to teachers' theories of effective teaching and learning was taken to be their description of effective teaching and learning for their respective focus classes. The coherence of such descriptions, as shown by the co-referencing and consistency of the descriptions of effective teaching and learning, may be taken to indicate the coherence of the theories of effective teaching and learning held by these teachers. Hence the teacher development program was directed towards improving the coherence of the descriptions of effective teaching and learning given by the participating teachers. In this way, new theories giving more coherent descriptions of effective teaching and learning were developed. This involved developing procedures for assessing both the connectedness and the consistency of descriptions of effective teaching and learning given by the teachers.

For the touchstone approach, the basic units of knowledge and beliefs to be dealt with are not individual claims, but whole sets of claims, or theories. Hence the personal theories of effective teaching and learning proposed by teachers must be dealt with as wholes. The emphasis must be on teachers providing a set of statements which give a complete description of effective teaching and learning for their respective focus classes. This contrasts with a foundationalist approach which stresses the analysis of descriptions of effective teaching and learning to find the underlying concepts, laws and principles, which define effective teaching and learning, that is, define a foundational theory of teaching and learning.

Individual statements should not be considered in isolation from the other statements describing effective teaching and learning. The important feature of any set of such statements is their coherence in describing effective teaching and learning. As previously argued, this coherence will be considered in terms of the connectedness and consistency of any set of statements purporting to describe effective teaching and learning.

The justification of knowledge claims and beliefs about teaching depends upon their coherence with the general fabric of our knowledge and beliefs about teaching. The justification of sets of knowledge claims and beliefs, or theories, about effective teaching and learning depends upon the coherence, the fit, of these knowledge claims about effective teaching and learning with the general background knowledge of teaching and learning of the teachers. Because the emerging theories and this background knowledge constantly interact, causing theories to be revised and the background knowledge to be reviewed, touchstone derived theories are in a continual state of revision. Other theories of teaching are in a constant state of review and revision. This implies that the teacher development program must be geared to participating teachers being able to review and revise their theories, and hence descriptions, of effective teaching and learning throughout the program, and to do so with the aim of making them increasingly coherent with their developing fabric of knowledge of effective teaching and learning.

Progress in Developing Theories of Teaching and Learning

Given the uniqueness of each participating teacher's experience as a teacher, it is likely that each teacher will have both different theories and background knowledge relating to effective teaching and learning. Given these differences, and if more generally acceptable theories of teaching and learning are to be developed, it is necessary to facilitate the sharing among teachers of these theories and backgrounds of knowledge. Such sharing requires the effective communication of the various theories held by individual teachers to other teachers. The clear articulation of such theories is necessary, and their intelligibility will be enhanced through communication between cooperating teachers. The intelligibility of the theories held by individual teachers and of the general background knowledge on effective teaching and learning shared by these teachers will be enhanced. The touchstone approach allows for communication and cooperation between teachers.

Progress for the teachers in the teacher development program is indicated by the enhanced intelligibility of the theories of effective teaching and learning advocated and supported.

Making Personal Theories of Teaching More Intelligible

Consider a set of statements which describes an episode of effective teaching and learning in a classroom. Under what conditions are these statements to be considered by a reader as intelligible, or, indeed, more intelligible? Let us begin by using an example from mathematics. Reimanian and Lobatchevskian geometries are alternative axiomatic systems of geometry to Euclidean geometry. They are, in part, due to the denial of Euclid's fifth axiom, or postulate, concerning the intersection, or non-intersection, of parallel lines. This denial, and the logical consequences of its adoption, although coherent, were, at first, considered implausible. Both systems, in particular their amendments of the fifth postulate, seemed implausible when considered against a background of everyday experience perceived in Euclidean space. An axiomatic system, and its consequences, may be considered implausible unless it gives an appearance of reasonableness in the arguments it uses, and the interpretations it supports and approves. Such a system may only be considered to be intelligible if the arguments, or reasoning, it uses, and the interpretations it approves, are plausible.

For a set of statements, two contributing factors for intelligibility are proposed: the set must be both coherent and plausible. Coherency may be considered in terms of the consistency of the statements and their connectedness. The coherence of a description is distinguished from its plausibility. A description may be strongly connected and highly consistent, but it may not be plausible. Thus a description of effective teaching and learning may be coherent, first, in the sense that the various semantic units, or sentences, in the description refer, through their objects, to one another and are therefore strongly connected, and, second, in that the properties and relations, the beliefs and values, attributed to these objects of the various sentences are consistent with one another. Such a description may not, however, be plausible.

This distinction between coherence and plausibility is stated by Johnson-Laird (1983) as follows:

> Coherence must be distinguished from plausibility, since a discourse may be perfectly coherent yet recount a bizarre sequence of events. The possibility of constructing a single mental model

depends on the principal factors of co-reference and consistency. Each sentence in a discourse must refer, explicitly or implicitly, to an entity referred to (or introduced) in another sentence, since only this condition makes it possible to represent the sentences in a single integrated model. Likewise, the properties and relations ascribed to the referents must be consistent, that is, compatible with one another and free from contradiction. Plausibility depends upon the possibility of interpreting the discourse in an appropriate temporal, spatial, causal and intentional framework. (1983: 370–1)

Hence teacher development will be indicated by an increasing intelligibility of the theories of effective teaching and learning proposed and supported by the particular teacher. Intelligibility requires both coherence and plausibility, whilst coherence can be considered in terms of connectedness and consistency. Indicators, and measures of these indicators, will be developed for the concepts of connectedness, consistency and plausibility and these will be used to indicate changes in intelligibility.

Communication and cooperation between teachers are implied by the adoption of a touchstone approach. It follows that communication and cooperation will be directed towards finding the overlap between the various competing theories of effective teaching and learning, and their implications. That is, agreement will be sought as to what is the overlap between any two theories, and to the most intelligible description of this overlap. Similarly, disagreements about the overlap of competing theories will need to be resolved to produce the most intelligible description, and hence the most intelligible theory of effective teaching and learning. Theory development proceeds according to agreement and disagreement amongst participating teachers.

This implies that agreements and disagreements between proposed solutions to the problem of describing effective teaching and learning should be emphasized. As previously suggested, this can be done by providing the opportunity for the teachers in the teacher development program to share, negotiate, review and revise their descriptions relating to effective teaching and learning. Each of these activities can be incorporated into the conduct of the teacher development program.

The touchstone approach concerns the overlap between competing theories. It concerns resolving the disagreements and integrating the agreements between competing theories. Thus '... educationists would give a very high priority to identifying and clearly stating their points of agreement and disagreement on matters of substance and method, and would address themselves to improving and devising techniques, based on their agreements, for frank and rigorous examination of their differences' (Walker and Evers, 1984: 28). In this way the development of educational theory and practice would take place through open, critical and intellectually developing discussion in which boundaries between, for example, the various disciplines, policy and practice, and research and practice, would begin to dissolve.

Implications for the Teacher Development Program

The teacher development program stresses the development of open, critical and intellectually developing discussions. This development is embodied within the procedures for conducting the program, procedures for sharing, negotiating, reviewing and revising descriptions of effective teaching and learning using groups of teacher participants. The membership of such groups is varied throughout the program in an attempt to reduce any limitations on discussions imposed by the professional and educational boundaries of the various teachers. In this way a climate of open, frank and critical discussion is encouraged.

Competition between theories arises when these theories propose different solutions to common problems. The resolution of disputes arising from competing theories, and therefore competing solutions, and the integration of new evidence with such theories, can proceed rationally and objectively because these theories and evidence deal with shared problems. Thus the resolution of conflicting theories of effective teaching and learning, and the integration of new evidence to form a new and more coherent solution, or theory, is a rational process based on the requirements for logical consistency, and is an objective process, because the theories being considered are all concerned with a common problem, namely describing effective teaching and learning. Touchstone theory, being based on the overlap between theories and hence on shared problems, can be developed objectively.

This implies that the teacher development program will be guided by the common problems shared by the teachers. The articulation and sharing of problems among participating teachers in order that common problems can be identified are emphasized. Once these have been established, the content and conduct of the program are directed towards their resolution. By continuing to focus on shared problems, the most objective solutions are obtained. The program gives ample opportunity for this articulating and sharing, and remains directed towards the problems shared by the teachers, in this case of describing effective teaching and learning. New knowledge and beliefs about teaching are developed in the process of finding a coherent solution to the shared problems of teaching. That is, knowledge of effective teaching and learning grows as participants in the teacher development program find coherent solutions to problems related to effective teaching and learning.

The program emphasizes solving shared problems as a means of acquiring and assimilating knowledge, rather than the acquisition of abstract theoretical knowledge. Whilst a set of readings was prepared for this program, these were not used with the aim of the participants acquiring the content of these readings as a body of knowledge. Rather, they were used to illustrate competing educational theories which, when considered in relation to the problem of describing effective teaching and learning, may give insights into this problem. Such competing theories may be used as ways of exploring the problem of describing effective teaching and learning, that is, as heuristics.

Whether a particular knowledge claim about teaching is accepted or rejected depends upon its coherence with the rest of our fabric of knowledge about teaching. But this particular claim also forms part of this general fabric of knowledge. In this sense the touchstone approach treats knowledge as self-referential. Hence a knowledge claim relating to effective teaching and learning would be accepted or rejected in terms of its coherence, its fit, with the general fabric of knowledge of effective teaching and learning, whilst it is recognized that this knowledge claim also forms part of this fabric of knowledge.

On this basis the teacher development program stresses the acceptance or rejection of a particular theory of effective teaching and learning on the basis of its coherence with the general fabric of knowledge of effective teaching of each participating teacher. This is done by referring all descriptions of effective teaching and learning by a teacher to the focus class of that teacher. Thus the teacher's knowledge of teaching and learning for the focus class is a vital component of the fabric of knowledge against which descriptions of effective teaching and learning are assessed for intelligibility.

Identifying the Touchstone of Competing Theories

How do we find the touchstone of competing themes? Suppose A, B and C are theories proposed for the solution of the same problem. That is, A, B and C are competing theories. In applying the touchstone approach to the development of a more coherent theory from these three competing theories, the agreements and disagreements between A, B and C must be identified.

This process may be begun by asking whether any two of A, B and C are clearly perceived to be similar. Suppose A and B are seen to be similar. To identify the crucial similarities and differences within this triad of theories, two key questions may be asked:

1   Because A and B are judged to be similar, in what way(s) are A and B in agreement?
2   In what way(s) are the pair A and B in disagreement from C?

The answer to the first question indicates the overlap between theories A and B, whilst the answer to the second question shows in what way(s) theories A and B do not overlap with theory C.

Suppose the statement of the answer to the first question is called the initial statement, and that for the second question the emergent statement. This nomenclature has been chosen to correspond with that used in eliciting repertory grids. The reason for this will become clear when the use of repertory grids is discussed later. By applying these two questions to the triad of theories A, B and C, an initial statement and an emergent statement can be elicited. The initial statement represents the overlap between the pair of theories A and B, and the emergent statement the disjunction between the pair A and B and theory C.

Suppose A_1, A_2, ..., A_n are competing theories. Then the number of triads of theories that can be formed from this set of n theories is $^nC_3$ (^{n}combination$_3$). For each of these triads an initial and an emergent statement may be elicited. In this case the set of $^nC_3$ initial statements represents the overlap between the pairs of elements from the triad, whilst the set of emergent statements represents the differences of each of the third elements of the triad from the pair of elements.

Consider competing theories A, B, C, D and E. These five theories will yield $^5C_3$, i.e. 10, triads. Each of these triads yields a pair of initial and emergent statements. Let these pairs of statements be C1, C2, ..., C10, and their initial and emergent statements be C1P1, C2P1, ... C10P1 and C1P2, C2P2, ..., C10P2 respectively. The competing theories, and the pairs of statements elicited from the triads of theories, can be represented as in Table 1.1.

If, for example, the pair of statements C1P1–C1P2 were derived from the triad A, B, C by comparing the pair A, B with C, then C1P1 represents the overlap between A and B, and C1P2 the difference of C from this pair. Thus statement C1P1 is in agreement with theories A and B, and in disagreement with theory C. On the other hand, statement C1P2 disagrees with theories A and B, but agrees with theory C. Such agreement and disagreement may be indicated by using a tick ($\sqrt{}$) or cross

Table 1.1. *Competing Theories*

Competing theories						
Initial statements	A	B	C	D	E	Emergent statements
C1P1						C1P2
C2P1						C2P2
C3P1						C3P2
C4P1						C4P2
C5P1						C5P2
C6P1						C6P2
C7P1						C7P2
C8P1						C8P2
C9P1						C9P2
C10P1						C10P2

(×) respectively, as in Table 1.2. This indicates that the pairs of theories shown in each of the possible theory triads listed below were used to generate the initial statement.

Triad	Pairs of statements elicited
ABC	C1P1–C1P2
BCD	C2P1–C2P2
CDE	C3P1–C3P2
DEA	C4P1–C4P2
EBA	C5P1–C5P2
CAE	C6P1–C6P2
DBA	C7P1–C7P2
ECB	C8P1–C8P2
ACD	C9P1–C9P2
BED	C10P1–C10P2

Table 1.2. Repertory Grid

Initial statement	A	B	C	D	E	Emergent statement
C1P1	√	√	X	X	√	C1P2
C2P1	√	X	√	√	√	C2P2
C3P1	√	X	X	√	√	C3P2
C4P1	√	√	√	X	√	C4P2
C5P1	X	√	√	X	√	C5P2
C6P1	√	√	√	√	X	C6P2
C7P1	X	√	√	√	X	C7P2
C8P1	X	√	√	√	X	C8P2
C9P1	√	X	√	X	√	C9P2
C10P1	√	√	X	X	√	C10P2

In the grid, for each pair of statements C1 to C10, two theories are not annotated. For example, theories D and E have not been annotated in relation to statements C1P1–C1P2. Each of these theories is now considered separately in terms of which statement, C1P1 or C1P2, is in closest agreement with the particular theory, D or E. Agreement with C1P1 is indicated by a tick (√) and with C1P2 by a cross (×). If, for example, D more nearly agrees with C1P2 and E with C1P1, this would be indicated as shown on the grid. All other remaining theories would be matched to the appropriate pairs of statements. An example of such matchings is shown in Table 1.1.

Hence the touchstone approach, when applied to competing theories using the triad method outlined above, can be used to develop a grid which indicates both the overlaps, or agreements, and disjunctions, or disagreements, between competing theories. For example, theories A, B and C overlap, and this overlap may be stated as C1P1, whilst theories C and D do not agree with C1P1 but with C1P2. Similarly, theories A and B are best interpreted as the sets of statements as listed below:

Theory A	Theory B
C1P1*	C1P1*
C2P1	C2P2
C3P1	C3P2
C4P1*	C4P1*
C5P2	C5P1
C6P1*	C6P1*
C7P2	C7P1
C8P2	C8P1
C9P1	C9P2
C10P1*	C10P1*

In terms of this grid the set of statements C1P1, C4P1, C6P1 and C10P1 represents the overlap between theories A and B.

This approach permits comparison of the agreements and disagreements between competing theories. It is based on a triad method and a logic of similarities and differences. It will be shown in Chapter 2 that the same method and logic are the basis of the triad method of repertory grid elicitation as developed from Kelly's (1955) *Psychology of Personal Constructs*.

What are the implications of these procedures for teacher development? The teacher development program may now be considered in terms of its implications for:

  i   conducting the teacher development program;
  ii the reading content of the program;
  iii monitoring and assessing changes in the intelligibility of the descriptions of effective teaching and learning given by participants;
  iv evaluating the overall effectiveness of the program.

First, as the program is focused on the problem of describing effective teaching and learning, it is organized around participating teachers' descriptions of effective teaching and learning for their focus classes. As the touchstone approach emphasizes the sharing of problems and their possible solutions, the program is organized so that the teachers are able to share their descriptions of effective teaching and learning with one another at regular intervals throughout the program.

The various descriptions of effective teaching and learning represent competing theories. The touchstone approach involves identifying agreements and disagreements between competing theories and attempting to resolve these by finding the most coherent alternative theory or resolution. The teacher development program provides opportunities for such agreements and disagreements to be identified and discussed, with a view to resolving them. These discussions, and the descriptions arising from them, can be used by the participating teachers to review and subsequently revise their personal descriptions of effective teaching and learning for their focus class.

The additional input provided by the reading content for the program can be used, both individually and jointly by the teachers, to explore various descriptions of effective teaching and learning. This exploration can be used as a basis for further sharing and discussion among the teachers, and for individual teachers to review and revise their descriptions of effective teaching and learning.

In summary, the conduct of the teacher development program entails:

    i   an emphasis on the participating teachers describing effective teaching and learning for their focus classes;

    ii these teachers recognizing the contrasting and competing theories of effective teaching and learning which may be implied by these descriptions;

    iii exploring, using the readings for the program, lecturer input and group and class discussions, the various theories and descriptions of effective teaching and learning which may be implied from these readings;

    iv sharing these descriptions and the theories they may imply with other participants;

    v reviewing these descriptions as a class, or in groups, and negotiating an agreed description for the class or group;

    vi individual participants reviewing and, if necessary, revising the description of effective teaching and learning for their focus class.

Thus the teacher development program uses the following learning activities for the teachers:

    i describing;

    ii recognizing;

iii exploring;
iv sharing;
v negotiating;
vi reviewing and revising.

Whilst these activities have been described as a sequence, it is not suggested that the various activities are mutually separable. Rather, this sequence is a way of construing the exploration and revision of the descriptions of effective teaching and learning of the participants, and, as such, can be used as a basis for planning the teacher development program. In the conduct of the program these activities may be perceived by the participants to enfold within one another. For example, sharing and negotiating activities may not appear separately, particularly if the group is committed to negotiating an agreed set of descriptions.

The program can be organized in the following phases, each associated with one of the activities given above:

i *the describing phase*: here teachers are concerned with describing effective teaching and learning for their focus class;

ii *the recognizing phase*: teachers are concerned with recognizing the contrasting descriptions and theories of effective teaching and learning, which may be implied within their descriptions of effective learning and teaching;

iii *the exploring phase*: using course readings, inputs from the lecturer in charge of the program, class and group discussions and individual reflection, alternative descriptions, and the competing theories of teaching and learning that these may imply, the various descriptions of teaching can be explored;

iv *the sharing phase*: the descriptions of effective teaching and learning, and the competing theories of teaching and learning these imply, are shared with other participants through group or whole class discussions;

v *the negotiating phase*: an attempt is made, either by groups of teachers or with the whole group, to negotiate an agreed description of effective teaching and learning;

vi *the reviewing and revising phase*: the agreed description of effective teaching and learning is considered by each teacher in relation to the description originally given by them for their focus class. This comparison is used to review and, if necessary, revise this description.

This sequence of activities may be seen as cyclic.

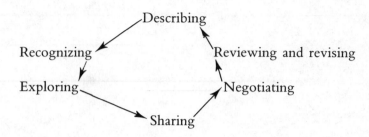

Describing

Recognizing

Reviewing and revising

Exploring

Negotiating

Sharing

The development of reading content of the program is described in detail in Chapter 3. In the case study on which this book is based each reading unit focuses on an approach to curriculum development. Each such unit was written to assist with the exploration phase of the program. It did so by emphasizing the contrasting theories of teaching and learning, which may be inferred from the particular approach to curriculum development. For example, the reading dealing with the student-centred approach to curriculum development emphasized the contrast between extrinsic (or instrumental) and intrinsic theories of motivation. Such contrasting theories were stated, usually, in terms of pairs of dichotomous or bipolar statements.

As the teacher development program is directed towards enhancing the intelligibility of the descriptions individual teachers give for effective teaching and learning, any evaluation of the program focused on the changes in intelligibility for individual teachers, rather than for program participants as a whole. Moreover, as each participant has a unique background and experience in teaching, and has concentrated on describing effective teaching and learning for their focus class, case studies for individual participants can be used as a basis for evaluating the effectiveness of the program in enhancing the intelligibility of the participants' theories of effective teaching and learning. A series of such case studies is given later in this book.

This evaluation must be distinguished from that of evaluating the approach taken to planning, conducting and evaluating this teacher development program. The evaluation of the approach to teacher development can be based on the teachers' responses to a series of evaluation questions. These responses can be considered in terms of the stated purposes of the teacher development program.

Chapter 2

Thinking about Effective Teaching

In the introduction it was argued that there are two major questions to be addressed by any theory of teaching: questions of learning, or construction of meaning, and of justification of claims to knowledge, beliefs and values. In Chapter 1 a touchstone approach was developed as a basis for justifying knowledge claims, beliefs, values and in this case descriptions of effective teaching and learning. The implications of this approach for the teacher development program were discussed.

In this chapter Kelly's theory of personal constructs (1955) is discussed as it describes the construction of meaning, and the implications of its adoption for the teacher development program are considered. In particular, the procedures for developing repertory grids, based on this theory, and for using these grids to monitor and assess changes in the intelligibility of the teachers' descriptions of effective teaching and learning are discussed. These discussions, and those of Chapter 1, are then used to develop a theoretical and procedural basis for the teacher development program.

Personal construct theory originates from the work of George A. Kelly as published in 1955 in *The Psychology of Personal Constructs*. Since then there has been a strong development of personal construct theory and its application to research and problem-solving. The general development and application of this theory are indicated, for example, by Bannister and Moir (1968), Maher (1969), Bannister (1970, 1977), Bannister and Fransella (1971, 1977, 1978), Thomas and Harri-Augstein (1977), Shaw (1980) and Bonarius, Holland and Rosenberg (1981).

The initial application of personal construct theory, and, in particular, repertory grid techniques, was to research and problems in the general fields of psychology and psychiatry, including training and counselling. Such applications are, for instance, reported by Benjafield and Adams-Webber (1975) (assimilative projections), Bieri (1966) (clinical and social judgment), Bonarius (1965) (role constructs), Brook (1979) (perceptions of vocational counselling), Cromwell and Caldwell (1962) (ratings of personal constructs of self and others), Duck (1973) (friendship formation), Gower (1977) (dimensions of intra-personal space), Honey (1979) (industrial and commercial training), Richardson and Weigel (1969) (marriage relationships), Smith, Hartley and Stewart (1978) (vocational guidance) and Tully (1976) (social work training).

From about 1975 there has been an increasing application of construct theory and repertory grid techniques to general theories and research procedures in education. These general developments are exemplified by the work of Bannister and Salmon (1975), Howe (1977), Shaw and Thomas (1978) and Pope and Shaw (1981). In addition, such theoretical developments and procedures have been applied to specific educational problems. The problems investigated include, in chronological order, the following:

i   attitudes to school subjects (Duckworth and Entwistle, 1974);
ii   the construing of reading by teachers and pupils (Beard, 1977);
iii the appraisal of teaching (Keen, 1977);
iv   monitoring and reflecting in teacher training (Pope, 1977);
v   developing students' learning skills (Keen, 1978);
vi   teaching styles in physics education (Keen, 1979);
vii staff-student interactions (Kevill and Shaw, 1980);
viii curriculum change (Olsen, 1980);
ix   changing constructs of postgraduate students (Phillips, 1980);
x   teacher influence in the classroom (Olsen, 1981);
xi   course evaluation (Kevill, Shaw and Goodacre, 1982);
xii creativity (Shaw and Gaines, 1982);
xiii innovations in science teaching (Olsen and Reid, 1982);
xiv teachers' beliefs and principles (Munby, 1983);
xv   teachers' epistemology and practice (Pope and Scott, 1984);
xvi information technology and teacher routines (Olsen, 1985);
xvii teachers' thinking about problems in practice (Lampert, 1985).

A discussion of the use of personal construct theory in investigating teaching and learning is included in Clandinin and Connelly (1986) as part of a wider analysis and interpretation of 'teachers' theories and beliefs', which focus on individual teachers' thoughts and actions, and which are called 'studies of the personal'.

Whilst personal construct theory and repertory grid procedures have been applied extensively to a variety of educational problems, they do not appear to have been used as part of the theoretical and procedural basis for teacher development as has been defined in terms of the enhancement of the intelligibility of teachers' descriptions of effective teaching and learning. In this case Kelly's (1955) theory of personal constructs is used, in conjunction with a touchstone approach to theory development, as such a basis.

Kelly's Theory of Personal Constructs

Repertory Grids

Repertory grids have their theoretical basis in personal construct theories. These theories, developed from the work of George A. Kelly, give comprehensive proposals relating to the construing of significant meaning by individuals. These proposals reflected a view of 'man as a personal scientist'. Kelly (1955) argued that each person constructs his own version of reality using a hierarchical or lattice system of constructs. People learn from experience when they are able to negotiate a viable position within their own version of reality, review it, sense it and refine it within their own world. Kelly saw the human being as a 'personal scientist', classifying, categorizing and theorizing about the world, and on these bases anticipating and hence acting on this world. Each person acts as a personal scientist, using himself as participative subject matter. The results of this participation are construed and interpreted in personally meaningful ways. To do this effectively, Kelly suggested that a conversational method must be used to bring into awareness the conceptual schemes constructed and held by the individual. The repertory grid has since been used as a method of developing such an awareness.

Personal constructs are the basic units of analysis in the theory of personality proposed by Kelly (1955). In this theory the major emphasis is on the ways each individual perceives their environment, the ways they interpret these perceptions in terms of existing personal constructs, and the consequent ways they behave towards the environment. Kelly proposes a view of man as being actively engaged in making sense of their world, and extending their experience of it. Within this view personal constructs are the dimensions that the individual uses to conceptualize experience. For each individual, personal constructs are used to forecast, and rehearse, events before their actual occurrence. For Kelly, man is a 'personal scientist', seeking to predict and control the course of events in which they participate.

Furthermore, Kelly (1955) proposed that each person has access to a limited number of constructs. These are used to evaluate the phenomena entailed within the experience of the individual. These phenomena, such as people, events, objects, ideas, purposes and institutions, are known as elements. Kelly (1955) further suggested that each personal construct was bipolar. That is, it was, for example, capable of being defined in terms of polar adjectives, such as 'good-bad', or polar phrases, such as 'makes me feel happy — makes me feel sad'.

Thus a repertory grid is a 'construction' matrix, which relates elements, representing the phenomena entailed in an individual's experience, and the bipolar personal constructs that the individual uses to conceptualize that experience.

Kelly's theory of personal constructs (1955) is based on a set of eleven corollaries. In the following section these corollaries are stated, and their implications for the teacher development program are considered, in particular, their implications for:

   i   planning and conducting the program;
   ii   developing a reading content for the program;
   iii   monitoring and assessing the changes in the intelligibility of participants' descriptions of teaching and learning; and
   iv   evaluating the program.

The corollaries which define Kelly's (1955) theory are:

1   *the construction corollary*: this proposes that a person anticipates events by construing their replication;
2   *the individuality corollary*: persons differ from each other in their construing of events;
3   *the organization corollary*: this assumes that each person characteristically evolves, for their convenience in anticipating events, a construction system embracing *ordinal* relationships between constructs; thus constructs are ways of ordering the world, and they are in turn organized into hierarchical or heterarchical frameworks, or into a lattice;
4   *the dichotomy corollary*: this suggests that a person's construction system is composed of a finite number of dichotomous constructs;
5   *the choice corollary*: a person chooses that alternative in a dichotomized construct through which they anticipate the greatest possibility for extension and definition of their system;
6   *the range corollary*: a construct is convenient for a finite number of events only;

7   *the experience corollary*: a person's construction system varies as they successfully construe the replication of events;

8   *the modulation corollary*: the variation in a person's construction system is limited by the permeability of the constructs within whose range of convenience the variants lie;

9   *the fragmentation corollary*: this states that a person may success-fully employ a variety of construction subsystems which are inferentially incompatible with one another;

10   *the commonality corollary*: this assumes that to the extent that one person employs a construction of experience, which is similar to that employed by another, his psychological processes are similar to those of the other person;

11   *the sociality corollary*: this proposes that, to the extent that one person construes the construction process of another, he may play a role in a social process involving the other person.

Implications for Teacher Development

Each of the eleven corollaries of Kelly's theory of personal constructs has implications for the conduct of the teacher development program.

The Construction Corollary

In proposing this corollary, Kelly assumes that a person comes to know their experience through successive interpretations of it. These interpreta-tions include images and thoughts. Whilst the person is free to inter-pret their experience in different ways, they are also bound by these interpretations.

The construction corollary involves four key concepts: anticipation, construct, event and replication. The notion of anticipation gives the theory of personal constructs its predictive and motivational features. Without the capacity to predict future events, it would be difficult for man to participate in an ever-changing world.

The act of construing is a process of abstracting in which one attributes properties to the ongoing stream of events which constitute experience. A person finds out about these events by attributing properties to these events: '... a person notes features in a series of elements which charac-terise some of the elements, and are particularly uncharacteristic of others' (Kelly, 1955: 50). For Kelly (1955), construed events are assumed to represent external events, and to do so through the abstraction of the perceived properties of these external events. Replication implies that an event that happens now has happened before, and will happen again. The replication of events is the basis of prediction.

Kelly's (1955) theory is concerned with psychological processes, and with the relationship of these processes with the processes entailed within personal experience. Within this process view, experience is conceptualized in terms of events. A person finds out about these events by attributing properties to them. Again, according to Kelly (1955), a person detects replicate aspects in a stream of events by construing the beginnings and endings of events. Moreover, the person does not construe the event, but the common intersection of properties of these events. Thus Kelly assumes a process view in which experience is conceptualized in terms of properties attributed to events.

The assumption of the construction corollary for the conduct of the teacher development program implies that:

i the program and its conduct must be conceptualized in terms of the learning processes involved;

ii the emphasis will be on the teachers describing effective teaching and learning for their focus class and on construing alternative interpretations of these descriptions;

iii the program should focus on the teachers' anticipated experience of effective teaching and learning with their focus class.

The Individuality Corollary

This corollary proposes that persons differ in their construal of events. That is, within a given context the same events are likely to be interpreted differently by different persons. This corollary supports the notion that the individual's own standpoint is the most fertile starting point for the process of understanding their conduct.

The teacher development program should emphasize, therefore, the teachers' personal descriptions of effective teaching and learning. These descriptions will be for the focus class of the teacher, and teacher development during the program will be indicated by changes in the intelligibility of these descriptions throughout the program.

The Organization Corollary

This assumes that each person evolves, for their convenience in anticipating experience, a set of personal constructs, which are ordinally related.

According to Kelly (1955), this system of constructs is hierarchically grounded. It evolves to minimize inconsistencies and incompatibilities. The function of this system is to assist the individual in anticipating events. When events are not successfully anticipated, the system of constructs is reviewed and revised.

This corollary has the following implications for the teacher development program.

i   The uniqueness of each individual's personal construct system (individuality corollary), particularly in terms of its ordination, implies that a student-centred approach will need to be taken for both the conduct of the program and the monitoring of teacher progress in the program.

ii The adjustment of individual systems of personal constructs, and hence of the descriptions of effective teaching and learning given by each teacher, proceeds through the elimination of inconsistencies and incompatibilities from this system. Hence emphasis will be given in the teaching development program to:

   — frequently applying the system to the descriptions of effective teaching and learning for the focus class;
   — using this to review and revise the construct system;
   — basing this review and revision on the elimination of inconsistencies and incompatibilities from this system;
   — using the exploration of alternative constructs and construct systems, gained through reading or discussions with other course participants, to assist with the elimination of inconsistencies and incompatibilities.

The elimination of inconsistencies and incompatibilities may be seen to be synonymous with an increase in intelligibility, and hence in the coherence and plausibility of the descriptions of effective teaching and learning.

The Dichotomy Corollary

This states that an individual's construct system consists of a finite number of dichotomous constructs. The dichotomy corollary implies that, for the teacher development program, each participant will explore alternative interpretations of their description of effective teaching and learning for their focus class using dichotomous or bipolar constructs. For Kelly a construct is:

the basic contrast between two groups. When it is imposed it serves to distinguish its elements and to group them. Thus the construct refers to the nature of the distinction one attempts to make between events, not the array in which events appear to stand when he gets through applying the distinction between each of them and all others. (Bannister, 1970: 13)

Hence the same act of construing that establishes some perceived similarity between two or more events also serves to distinguish them from other events. In this sense each construct is both an integrating and differentiating process.

A construct is a process, and must be distinguished from a concept.

A construct is a way in which some things are seen as being alike yet different from others. The idea of a relevant contrast and a limited range of applicability or convenience is not involved in the notion of a concept, but is essential to the definition of a construct. Sometimes concepts are also regarded as ways in which certain things are actually alike and really different from other things. This use suggests the concept is being regarded as a feature of the nature of things/an inherent categorization of reality. The idea of a construct does not carry with it any such assumption, but rather is seen as an interpretation imposed upon events, not carried in the events themselves. The reality of a construct is in its use by a person as a device for making sense of the world, and so anticipating it more fully. It must be stressed that all invented dichotomies, however widely agreed (large-small), specifically annotated (base-treble), or scientifically approved (acid-alkali) are constructs — useful conventions, not facts of nature. (Bannister and Moir, 1968: 25–6)

Furthermore,

... it must be understood that the personal constructs abstract similarity and difference, simultaneously. One cannot be abstracted without implying the other. For a person to treat two incidents as different is to imply that one of them appears to be like another he knows. Conversely, for a person to treat two incidents as similar is to imply that he contrasts both of them with at least one other incident he knows. We intend this to be considered as an essential feature of the personal construct by means of which we hope to understand the psychology of human behaviour. (Kelly, 1969: 102–3)

For a construct, both similarity and difference are essential. For Kelly, this dichotomous nature of constructs is an essential feature of the way in which experience is interpreted. Each construct represents a bipolar distinction.

The implications for the teacher development program are:

  i   the exploration of the differences and similarities within, and between, descriptions of effective teaching and learning;
 ii   using these explorations to elicit bipolar constructs as devices for interpreting these descriptions;
iii   basing the eliciting of these constructs on contrasting the similarities and differences of a group of at least three semantic units of descriptions of effective teaching and learning;
 iv   suggesting, through reading, discussion and personal reflection, alternative bipolar constructs, which' could be used in interpreting descriptions of effective teaching and learning.

The Choice Corollary

This indicates that for each bipolar construct the individual will choose that pole which is anticipated to give the best possibility of both defining and extending their personal construct system. The predominant aim is to define and extend the personal construct system to optimize the anticipation of events in such a way as to meet the needs, interests and purposes of the individual.

This process of choice will be enhanced by the acquaintance of each teacher, through personal reflection, discussion and reading, with a wide range of bipolar constructs, which may be applied to their descriptions of effective teaching and learning. The teacher will choose those constructs which define and expand their personal construct systems, in ways that meet their future needs, interests and purposes. That is, the choice participants make among constructs will be based on their anticipated needs, interests and purposes in relation to effective teaching and learning. The future expectation of the participants will be a major influence in their review and revision of their construct systems. Hence the teacher development program should present alternative constructs, which take into account the probable future needs and purposes of the participants. As the paricipants all expect to gain greater responsibility for the administration of education, the program should emphasize constructs relating to a wider perspective of education appropriate to these responsibilities.

The Range Corollary

This corollary states that any given construct is convenient or useful for a finite range of events only. That is, the range of experience to which a particular construct can apply is limited. For a person to anticipate successfully, they must locate an event within a dichotomous construct that is hierarchically integrated with other constructs. The located event will then be perceived in particular ways, as determined by its location within this hierarchy.

The choice of contrasting poles for a construct will limit the events to which the construct can be meaningfully applied. Thus the construct male/female is limited to events for which the similarities and differences between males and females are significant in that they assist in anticipating future experience. The applicability of particular constructs will be restricted, therefore, to specific contexts. The transfer of the application of a construct from one context, say primary education, to another, such as secondary education, may require special strategies and, in particular, the development of a superordinate construct.

This indicates that the constructs employed by the teachers may only be applicable to a limited experience of teaching and learning. In this case teachers will only be able to give restricted descriptions and interpretations of effective teaching and learning. To expand the construct systems used by the teachers, it will be necessary, as well as providing a wide range of alternative constructs, to encourage them to develop superordinate constructs. This suggests discussing, and reflecting upon, constructs of wider applicability, and hence of a more general, and usually abstract, level. Provision must be made for the presentation of such constructs during the program.

The Experience Corollary

This corollary proposes that a person's constructive system varies as he successfully construes the replication of events. That is, successful construal occurs when the rehearsal of the event, such as teaching a particular lesson, in terms of a particular construct or constructs, allows the successful anticipation of the event. Thus, by reflecting on the lesson in terms of a particular set of constructs, the teacher is able to anticipate what will happen during the lesson. This capacity to anticipate is enhanced by rehearsal.

In addition, the individual, in rehearsing, adopts the system of constructs used on the basis of its success or failure in anticipating experience. This indicates that learning is anticipatory, involving the development of constructs which yield predictive success. A student's capacity to recognize, review, test and revise constructs in terms of their predictive success is, for these reasons, essential. That is, a critically reflective capacity must be developed.

This implies that the planning and conduct of the teacher development program should emphasize the development of this capacity by stressing predictive success. This is done by referring the interpretation of the teachers' descriptions of effective teaching and learning to their focus class, and testing and revising these interpretations, and the constructs on which they are based, in terms of their continuing experience with this focus class.

The Modulation Corollary

This corollary proposes that the variation in a person's constructive system is limited by the permeability of the constructs within whose range of convenience the variants lie. Personal construct theory emphasizes the anticipation and prediction of experience. The focus is on the ability of the person to invent and reinvent construct systems that give both order and meaning to experience. For such theories, change is conceptualized as a process instrinsic to a person's attempts to give order and meaning to experience. In this case, the two critical questions are: (i) under what conditions can change occur, and (ii) when change does occur, what changes in a person's construction system?

According to the organization corollary, an individual's system of constructs is hierarchically organized. For a hierarchy, each level is subsumed by a higher, and more integrative, level. The higher the level of the construct within the hierarchy of the system of constructs, the higher the degree of abstractness of the form or structure of the construct. That is, the degree of abstractness of the structure, or form of the construct, is determined by its relative position within the vertical organization of the hierarchy.

Within this hierarchy each construct will be linked to at least one other construct. The more inferential links a construct possesses, the more extensive is the array of implicated constructs. That is, there is a greater number of possible implied constructs from a given construct. Applying this construct to a particular incident makes possible a wide range of implied meanings or interpretations. The construct give rise to a wide range of possible interpretations. In addition, the greater the range of possible interpretations which can be drawn from a particular construct, the greater its flexibility in subsuming or enfolding the full range of interpretations of a variety of events.

This property of a construct both to yield a wide range of interpretations and to subsume or enfold interpretations of a variety of events is called its permeability. A given construct in an individual's construct system may be more 'abstract', that is, higher in the hierarchy, less inferentially linked and less flexible in encapsulating alternative interpretations. The permeability of the constructs within a person's construct system limits the range and flexibility of interpretations available from this construction system.

On these arguments an individual's perception of a particular incident will be limited by the permeability of their system of constructs. A lack of permeability may prevent an individual from giving possible interpretations of this incident. In this case the person may have to modify or adjust their construction system so that the incident can be more effectively construed for predictive success. This can only be done if there is at least one construct which is sufficiently permeable to accommodate at least some interpretations of the incident. Thus the relative permeability of the construct system determines what can be varied or altered within the system. A highly rigid, impermeable system has little capacity for modification. An open, highly permeable system has considerable capacity for the interpretation and accommodation of experience.

The assumption of a holistic epistemology implies that teacher development will be concerned with open-minded and intellectually critical reflection and inquiry. This approach to teacher development is supported, therefore, by the development of open and highly permeable personal construct systems. The teacher development program should make available to teachers highly permeable, alternative constructs and construct systems for reflection and discussion. These systems must be able to accommodate, at least in part, the experiences of the participants in teaching their focus class. That is, at least one construct must be able to yield a plausible interpretation of the teacher's experience in teaching their focus class. This implies that the program should begin with the interpretations the participants give for effective teaching and learning for their focus classes, and the constructs these embody. These interpretations and constructs may then be adjusted and modified throughout the program, ensuring that a degree of permeability is retained and, desirably, enhanced. Thus the monitoring of the progress of teachers throughout the program should be in terms of the focus class. Care needs to be taken to monitor individual construct systems, formally through repertory grid analysis and informally through class and group discussions, for their adjustment towards a more permeable, open system. Emphasizing heuristic discussions in the program facilitates this informal monitoring.

The Fragmentation Corollary

This states that a person may employ, successfully, a variety of construction subsystems, which are inferentially incompatible with one another. That is, predictive success may be obtained using a particular system of personal constructs, despite some of the underlying constructs conflicting. An individual may tolerate such incompatibility provided this does not interfere with their dominant needs, interests and purposes. If these needs, interests and purposes were to change, these conflicting constructs could not be tolerated. They would be incompatible with the individual's perspective of the future. In this case mutual adaptation of the personal construct system, and this perspective, to eliminate these conflicts would occur.

This suggests that the conduct of the teacher development program must take into account the needs, interests and purposes of the participants throughout the program. As these change, so will the constructs used by the participants to interpret their descriptions of effective teaching and learning for their focus class. This implies a student-centred approach to the planning and conduct of the teacher development program, and based on the focus class of each participant.

The Commonality Corollary

This corollary proposes that to the extent that one person employs a construction system which is similar to that used by another, their psychological processes are similar to that other person. Thus, if the participants in the teacher development program use similar constructs, their psychological processes are similar. When, for example, a group of teachers negotiates an agreed set of constructs, and applies these to their descriptions of effective teaching and learning, it is assumed that each participant is using the same psychological processes. This corollary has particular importance for the conduct of group or class negotiation during the teacher development program.

The Sociality Corollary

This corollary proposes that to the extent to which one person construes the construction process of another, they may play a role in a social process involving the other person. In this context Kelly defines a role as follows: 'A role is a psychological process based upon the role player's construction of aspects of the construction system of those with whom he attempts to join in social enterprise' (Kelly, 1955: 97).

Thus the planning and conduct of the teacher development program should facilitate and support social relating. It should enable all teachers to construe the construction processes of all other teachers. It must enable each participant to examine and reflect upon the variety of ways in which effective teaching and learning will be construed by other teachers. This is facilitated by sharing descriptions of effective teaching and learning, and the construct systems used to interpret them, with all teachers in the program.

Thus the implications of these corollaries for the planning and conduct of the teacher development program are as follows:

i   the program, and its conduct, must be conceptualized in terms of the learning processes involved (construction corollary);

ii   the emphasis should be on the participant describing effective teaching and learning for their focus class, and on construing interpretations of these descriptions (construction corollary);

iii   the program should emphasize the teacher's anticipated experience of effective teaching and learning with their focus class (construction corollary);

iv   the program should emphasize the teacher's personal descriptions of effective teaching and learning for their focus class (individuality corollary);

v   a student-centred approach to the conduct of the program, and the monitoring of participant progress throughout this program, must be adopted (individuality and organization corollaries);

vi   an emphasis on the frequent application of the teacher's construct system to their descriptions of effective teaching and learning for their focus class (organization corollary);

  vii using this application to review and revise these construct systems (organization corollary);

 viii basing this review and revision on the elimination of inconsistencies and incompatibilities from these systems (organization corollary);

   ix using the exploration of alternative constructs and construct systems, gained either through reading or through discussions with other course participants, to assist with the elimination of inconsistencies and incompatibilities (organization corollary);

    x emphasizing the exploration of differences and similarities within, and between, descriptions of effective teaching and learning (dichotomy corollary);

   xi using these explorations to elicit bipolar constructs as devices for interpreting these descriptions (dichotomy corollary);

  xii basing the eliciting of these constructs on contrasting the similarities and differences of groups consisting of at least three semantic units, usually sentences, of the descriptions of effective teaching and learning (dichotomy corollary);

 xiii suggesting alternative bipolar constructs which could be used to interpret these descriptions of effective teaching and learning (dichotomy corollary);

  xiv the alternative constructs presented should recognize the anticipated needs, interests and purposes of individual participants (choice corollary);

   xv the alternative constructs provided, discussed and reflected upon should have a wide range of applicability, and should support the development of superordinate constructs (range corollary);

  xvi emphasizing the development of the teacher's capacity to predict likely success in providing effective teaching and learning for their focus class by referring descriptions of effective teaching and learning, and their interpretations, to the focus class, and by reviewing and revising these interpretations, and the constructs on which they are based, in terms of the teacher's continuing experience with their focus class (experience corollary);

 xvii open-minded, and intellectually critical, inquiry should be encouraged (modulation corollary);

xviii the alternative constructs provided during the program should be highly permeable, but should accommodate descriptions of effective teaching and learning for the focus classes (modulation corollary);

xix basing the program initially on descriptions of effective teaching and learning for the focus classes (modulation corollary);

xx using group discussion and negotiations to achieve commonality of construct systems, where this is considered desirable (commonality corollary);

xxi facilitating social relating during the program to help participants construe, and reflect upon, the construction systems of other participants (sociality corollary);

xxii recognizing the changing needs, interests and purposes, particularly as these reflect conflicts within teachers' construction systems, by adopting a student-centred approach to the planning and conduct of this program (fragmentation corollary).

From this summary it follows that the teachers in the program will be involved in:

i describing effective teaching and learning;
ii recognizing alternative, contrasting descriptions of effective teaching and learning;
iii exploring alternative descriptions of effective teaching and learning;
iv sharing alternative descriptions of effective teaching and learning;
v negotiating alternative descriptions of effective teaching and learning;
vi reviewing and revising alternative descriptions of effective teaching and learning.

There is strong support, also, for basing the program on the descriptions of effective teaching and learning of the focus classes of the teachers, for developing constructs using a triad method, and for emphasizing the elimination of inconsistencies and incompatibilities of construct systems.

Implications for Reading Program

The acceptance of the corollaries of Kelly's (1955) personal construct theory has implications for the selection, and use, of the reading content of the teacher development program. As previously argued, these corollaries in general, and the organization corollary in particular, suggest the exploration of alternative construct systems. The purpose of this exploration is to eliminate inconsistencies and incompatibilities from the personal construct systems of the teachers in the teacher development program. This exploration is assisted if the teachers study, reflect upon and discuss readings which emphasize a range of plausible constructs. These need to be plausible in that the participants are able to use these constructs to develop interpretations of effective teaching and learning for the focus classes, which fit and are coherent with their experience of teaching that focus class. This is supported by implications drawn from the choice corollary.

In using the program readings participants explore the differences and similarities of various ways of describing effective teaching and learning. The readings provided should emphasize a range of such possibilities. They should be used by the participants to develop bipolar constructs, which stress the similarities and differences of descriptions of effective teaching and learning; in particular, highlighting the similarities and differences between various descriptions of effective teaching and learning should be encouraged. This is supported by implications arising from the dichotomy corollary.

From the range corollary it has been concluded that the alternative constructs provided by the program readings should have a wide range of applicability, and should encourage the development of superordinate constructs. This implies that the readings should consider effective teaching and learning at a general level, and for a wide range of teaching-learning contexts. That is, readings should not consider teaching or curriculum development, for example, for a particular subject only, or for primary education only; they should consider general principles and procedures relating to teaching and learning. The consideration of such general principles and procedures should enhance the range of circumstances to which the readings can be applied, and the possibility of the teachers developing more general, or superordinate, constructs with which to interpret their descriptions of effective teaching and learning.

It has been argued that the modulation corollary supports the encouragement of open-minded and intellectually critical inquiry. The readings supplied to the participants should reflect such an approach to inquiry. In particular, they should be open in the sense of not supporting any particular bias in approaches to teaching and learning, and should stress the need to be intellectually critical of the arguments used. The readings should reflect an open-minded and intellectually critical style of inquiry.

Moreover, and as suggested by the modulation corollary, the alternative constructs provided in the readings should be highly permeable. That is, the constructs should enable the teachers to develop a range of possible interpretations rather than be limited to a small number of highly specified interpretations. At the same time these interpretations should accommodate the descriptions of effective teaching and learning given by the teachers.

In summary, the readings supplied to the teachers should discuss a wide range of plausible alternative bipolar constructs by emphasizing the similarities and differences of various educational perspectives when applied to the problem of describing effective teaching and learning. The readings should be written in a style which encourages open-minded and critical inquiry, and the development of superordinate constructs.

Implications for Assessment and Evaluation

It has been argued that acceptance of the corollaries of Kelly's (1955) theory of personal constructs implies a student-centred approach to the conduct, monitoring and evaluation of the teacher development program. Thus monitoring and assessing the changes in the intelligibility of the descriptions of effective teaching and learning for the focus classes of individual teachers will be undertaken during the program. This pro-cedure is supported by implications drawn from the construction, individuality and organization corollaries.

As previously discussed, the teacher development program empha-sizes contrasting the similarities and differences of various descriptions of effective teaching and learning to produce sets of bipolar constructs. This emphasis is in accord with the organization, dichotomy, choice, range, experience and modulation corollaries. The descriptions of effec-tive teaching and learning for the focus class of a participant, and the bipolar constructs which can be elicited from these descriptions, may be used to develop repertory grids on effective teaching and learning. The analysis and interpretation of these grids can be used to monitor the changes in the intelligibility of these descriptions.

As the corollaries of Kelly's (1955) theory of personal constructs have been shown to imply a student-centred approach to the teacher develop-ment program, evaluation of the program must be in terms of the changes to the individuals participating in the program. As the program is directed towards changing the intelligibility of the descriptions partici-pants give for effective teaching and learning for their focus classes, these changes should be the basis on which the program is evaluated. For these reasons the program should be evaluated using an individual case study approach for a selection of participants. The case studies should concen-trate on the changes in the intelligibility of the above descriptions. In addition, the effectiveness of the program in meeting its purposes for the participants will need to be evaluated.

The Development and Analysis of Repertory Grids

As repertory grids are to be used to monitor changes in the intelligibility of teachers' descriptions, we must now consider the development of repertory grids and their use in interpreting the teachers' descriptions of effective teaching. A repertory grid is a matrix of elements and bipolar constructs. The grid is developed, first, by choosing a set of elements, and, second, by using these elements to elicit a set of bipolar constructs.

A repertory grid is usually developed in relation to a specific problem, need, issue or task. The elements are chosen by the individual developing the grid. They must be personally important and meaningful to that individual. The total set of elements chosen must be representative of the normal discourse associated with the item being considered. If, for example, the problem to be considered is that of describing effective teaching and learning for a focus class, the elements chosen may, for instance, be statements describing effective teaching and learning for that class. This set of statements should be representative of the entire discourse, which relates to teaching and learning for that class. As well as being representative, the set of elements chosen should be as specific in meaning as possible. In addition, the elements should be homogeneous in the sense of being similarly defined. If, for example, the elements to be chosen are guidelines for effective teaching and learning for the focus class, then each must fit a common notion of a guideline. An element stated as a stipulative rule, rather than a guideline, would not be acceptable as being homogeneous with the remaining elements.

In the development of a repertory grid the elements may be supplied to those concerned. For the example given above, those developing repertory grids based on guidelines for effective teaching and learning could be supplied with a set of such guidelines. Similarly, a pool of elements could be supplied, and selections of elements made from this pool. Such a pool could, for instance, be established through a literature review for effective teaching and learning, by surveying a population of teachers, or through discussions with a group of teachers.

The choice of method for choosing elements depends upon (i) the purposes for developing the repertory grid, and (ii) the knowledge, experience and skills of those developing the grid. If, for example, the aim is to produce a repertory grid for guidelines for effective teaching and learning for the purpose of having a group of teachers explore effective teaching and learning in relation to the teaching of a particular skill, then supplying a predetermined set of guidelines would seem justified. Alternatively, if the purpose is to have teachers develop skills and experience in exploring a wide range of alternative guidelines for effective teaching and learning, allowing these teachers to develop such guidelines would seem to be appropriate, provided that they had the knowledge and skills to do so. A range of methods has been developed for generating constructs. Depending upon the purposes for developing the repertory grid, and the context in which it is being developed, the constructs may be either supplied or elicited. In this case only procedures for eliciting constructs which were used in the case study are given.

For the full context form, each element is written on a card and displayed before the individual. The individual is asked to prepare important senses in which groups of the elements are alike. Two elements are then selected, and the way these are similar is recorded. Further cards are then sequentially added to the group. As each element is added, the individual is asked whether this element belongs to the same category as the first two. If not, then the difference is used as a basis for stating the contrast pole, and the similarity of the first two for stating the implicit pole. This procedure is continued until sufficient constructs have been generated.

For the sequential form of this procedure, the elements are represented as triads, as for the minimum context form, rather than as a group, as for the full context form. The procedure, however, differs from that of the minimum context form in that the selection of the triads of elements proceeds systematically by changing the elements of the triad one at a time and sequentially. If the first triad of elements is 1, 2, 3, then the second is formed by replacing 1 with 4, and so on.

In investigating how teachers construe effective teaching and learning, the minimum context, the full context and the sequential form are valid procedures. Each of these is based upon the triad method of eliciting constructs. Kelly based the triad method on his views on how constructs are first formed. But as the constructs being elicited are already established in the individual's repertoire, there appears to be no reason why three elements need to be used. More explicit contrasts may be obtained by asking the individual for the opposite or contrast of the likeness which had been discerned between any two elements. Thus two elements, or a dyadic procedure, can be used. This procedure is simpler to use than the triadic method. For each dyad, an important way in which the elements are similar and an important way in which they are different are identified. These indicate the implicit and contrasting poles respectively.

As it was planned to limit the number of elements in each grid for each teacher to not less than six and not more than ten, and as these elements were to be statements describing effective teaching and learning for the focus class of each teacher, a sequential form procedure using triads of elements was considered appropriate for eliciting constructs.

In the development of a repertory grid we begin by developing the elements and constructs. The problem or issue to be investigated is represented by a set of elements. From these elements a set of constructs is elicited. The grid is a matrix formed from these elements and constructs.

The elements of the grid are always items of personal experience. As such, they can be used to elicit constructs for the grid. The relevance of the grid to the purpose for which it is being used will depend upon the types of elements it contains. The best set of elements is that which enables the person to explore their own patterns of personal meaning, to become more fully aware of their patterns of thoughts and feelings, as these relate to their purposes.

A personal construct may be seen as a dimension of personal meaning, and the system of personal constructs defines a person's psychological space. The structure of personal meaning within which the items of experience acquire their significance, one in relation to the other, defines this space. If two items of experience are thought to be similar, then they lie close to one another in the personal construct system. The use of words such as 'space', 'structure' and 'lie close' indicates that the idea of a system of personal constructs is closely analogous with that of physical space. This analogy must be recognized and retained only as long as it is helpful in investigating personal meaning.

The following exercise was helpful for the teachers in gaining an initial understanding of how a repertory grid is developed.

Think of six people who you have recently taught. Obtain six cards of say 10cm × 6cm. Using these cards write one of your learners' names on each of the six cards. Shuffle them, and label then E1 to E6.

Deal out cards E1, E2 and E3 and consider each of the learners named by these cards, in turn. Try to imagine yourself in a learning/teaching situation with each of them in turn. Now think about them as learners. Which two of the three are most alike as learners, and which one is most different as a learner from the other two? Put the two 'similar learners' together and separate the card for the 'different learner' from this pair.

Table 2.1. *Matrix for Repertory Grid*

	E1	E2	E3	E4	E5	E6	
C1P1							C1P2
C2P1							C2P2
C3P1							C3P2
C4P1							C4P2
C5P1							C5P2
C6P1							C6P2

On paper write a brief description of what it is about the pair which leads you to put them together. Label this C1P1 (Construct 1, pole 1). When you have done this write a brief description, on a second piece of paper, of what it is about the third person that makes them different as a learner. Label this C1P2.

Put CP1, CP2 and cards E1, E2 and E3 aside. Deal out E4, E5 and E6 and repeat the procedure. This procedure will then yield C2P1 and C2P2.

Repeat the procedure using the triads of cards such as E1, E3 and E5, and E2, E4 and E6 thus generating C3P1 and C3P2, C4P1 and C4P2, C5P1 and C5P2, and C6P1 and C6P2. These construct cards should then be displayed as follows:

> C1P1 – C1P2
> C2P1 – C2P2
> C3P1 – C3P2
> C4P1 – C4P2
> C5P1 – C5P2
> C6P1 – C6P2

These construct cards display ways you think and feel about learners. The constructs so obtained, and the elements they refer to, form the matrix of a repertory grid. This matrix may be displayed as in Table 2.1.

For the first construct (C1P1–C1P2), consider each element E1–E6 in turn. Each element is assigned to one pole or other of the construct. Thus if E1 is considered to most nearly fit C1P1 then this element is assigned to this pole of the first construct. Assignment to the first (emergent) pole, C1P1, is indicated by a tick ($\sqrt{}$), whilst assignment to the second (implicit) pole, C1P2, is shown by a cross (×). In this way all elements E1–E6 are assigned to one or other pole of the first construct giving the typical pattern (Table 2.2).

The remaining constructs are similarly assigned to each of the elements enabling the grid to be completed (Table 2.2).

In this example the steps taken to elicit the repertory grid agree with those proposed by Thomas and Harri-Augstein (1985).

1 Decide upon the purpose of the grid.
2 Identify the types of elements which best allow this purpose to be achieved.
3 Elicit the elements.
4 Elicit a personal construct.
5 Assign the elements to the construct.
6 Elicit further constructs and assign the elements to them.

A range of procedures is available for analyzing and interpreting the repertory grid. In this case a correlation analysis based upon matching pairs of columns or rows will be described. With this procedure a correlation matrix can be completed for the elements, and a further correlation matrix developed for the constructs.

The repertory grid, when completed, gives a matrix of ticks ($\sqrt{}$) and crosses (×). This matrix may be displayed as in Table 2.2.

For elements A and B, count the number of occasions when the assignments ($\sqrt{}$ or ×) match for the various constructs. In the example there are four instances of this matching. This number is then entered in the A/B space for the correlation matrix of elements in Table 2.3. This procedure is repeated until all pairings of elements have been exhausted. The same procedure is then repeated for the constructs, and the correlation matrix of Table 2.4 completed. These matrices give an indication of the pairs of elements and pairs of constructs which are closely related. An inspection of Table 2.4 indicates, for example, a high correlation between elements A and C and constructs 1 and 5.

As previously argued, the intelligibility of descriptions of effective teaching and learning can be considered in terms of their coherence and plausibility. Coherence is concerned with the consistency and connectedness of the set of statements used to describe effective teaching and

Table 2.2. Repertory Grid

Construct	A	B	C	D	E	F	G	H	I	J	Construct / Emergent pole
					Elements (Statements)						
1	✓	X	✓	✓	X	✓	X	X	✓	X	
2	✓	✓	✓	X	X	✓	✓	✓	X	✓	
3	X	✓	X	✓	✓	X	X	X	X	✓	
4	X	✓	X	✓	X	✓	✓	X	✓	X	
5	✓	X	✓	✓	✓	X	X	X	✓	X	
6	X	✓	X	X	X	✓	X	X	X	✓	
7	✓	✓	X	✓	X	✓	✓	✓	✓	✓	
8	✓	X	✓	X	X	✓	✓	✓	X	X	
9	X	✓	X	✓	✓	✓	X	X	X	✓	
10	✓	✓	✓	X	✓	X	X	✓	X	X	

Table 2.3. Correlation Matrices for Repertory Grids: Correlation Matrix for Elements

Elements	A	B	C	D	E	F	G	H	I	J
A		4	8	5	3	5	5	7	6	2
B			2	5	5	5	4	5	2	8
C				3	4	5	6	7	6	2
D					6	4	3	2	7	5
E						2	3	3	5	5
F							7	4	5	5
G								7	6	4
H									3	5
I										2
J										

Table 2.4. Correlation Matrices for Repertory Grids: Correlation Matrix for Constructs

Constructs	1	2	3	4	5	6	7	8	9	10
1		4	3	6	8	4	7	6	4	4
2			3	4	2	6	5	8	4	6
3				2	5	7	4	1	9	4
4					6	4	5	6	4	4
5						2	5	4	4	6
6							5	4	8	4
7								5	5	3
8									6	5
9										4
10										

learning, and hence with the elements of the repertory grids developed by participating teachers. The plausibility of these descriptions is concerned with their practical reasonableness. This is assessed in terms of the interpretations the teacher places upon the particular descriptions of effective teaching and learning. These interpretations are reflected in the system of constructs, or bipolar statements, developed from the given set of descriptive statements or elements.

Each repertory grid consists of a set of elements and a set of bipolar statements or constructs. The elements are sentences describing effective teaching and learning, whilst the bipolar statements (constructs) have been derived from these elements using the triad method as previously described. For each such grid, correlation matrices for both the elements and the bipolar statements (constructs) may be completed.

Correlation of Elements

Consider the repertory grid shown in Table 2.5.

In this grid a tick ($\sqrt{}$) indicates that the element most nearly matches, in meaning, the initial statement, whilst a cross ($\times$) indicates that it matches more closely with the emergent statement. Placing a tick ($\sqrt{}$) in the box for element C and the bipolar statements C3P1–C3P2 indicates that element C matches more closely with the statement C3P1. A cross would indicate a matching with C3P2, the emergent statement.

As elements A and B match for five of the six bipolar statements with the same pole of the statement, that is, with the initial statement, there is a high correlation between elements A and B. The number of such matches is taken as a measure of the correlation between the elements. In this case the correlation between A and B is five.

Correlation scores for all possible pairs of elements can then be computed, and represented on the matrix (Table 2.6).

Consistency of descriptions. If, in the above grid, all elements were matched with the initial poles of the bipolar statements in all cases, then the grid would contain only ticks ($\sqrt{}$), and all correlation scores would be six. In this case the given description of effective teaching and learning can be interpreted, without exception, in terms of the initial poles of the set bipolar statements. That is, the elements of the grid can be interpreted entirely within the perspective of effective teaching and learning defined by the set of the initial pole statements. In this sense the elements of the grid provide a description which is consistent with this perspective and, in particular, does not contradict it. Thus the description provided by

Table 2.5. Repertory Grid

Bipolar statements	Elements						Bipolar statements
Initial statement	A	B	C	D	E	F	Emergent statement
C1P1	✓	✓	X	✓	X	✓	C1P2
C2P1	✓	✓	X	✓	X	X	C2P2
C3P1	✓	✓	✓	X	✓	✓	C3P2
C4P1	✓	✓	✓	X	✓	✓	C4P2
C5P1	✓	X	X	✓	✓	X	C5P2
C6P1	✓	✓	✓	✓	X	✓	C6P2

Table 2.6. Correlation Matrix of Elements

Elements	A	B	C	D	E	F
A		5	3	4	3	4
B			4	3	2	5
C				1	4	5
D					1	2
E						3
F						

elements A to F is consistent with the perspective of effective teaching and learning depicted by statements C1P1, C2P1, C3P1, C4P1, C5P1 and C6P1. Where correlation scores are less than the maximum possible score (in this case six), then the elements do not give a fully consistent description. The degree of consistency of the description provided by the elements is indicated by the overall level of the correlation scores in the matrix.

Connectedness of the elements. If the elements of a repertory grid are to give a coherent description of effective teaching and learning, they must not only be consistent, as described above, but the elements should refer to one another. Through such co-referencing, the elements can form a coherent network or description. For this to be the case, the referents of each element must refer to the referents of at least one other element in the grid. In this way all elements connected in the grid can be linked through co-reference.

Consider a repertory grid with the following elements as descriptions of effective teaching and learning.

A   Good teaching provides students with the opportunity to measure their progress.
B   Good teaching involves individual and group work, equally.
C   Good teaching involves communicating in a manner suitable for the maturity level of the child.
D   Good teaching involves negotiation of the curriculum with students.
E   Good teaching encourages the development of self-motivation.
F   Good teaching draws on a wide range of experiences and resources.

Table 2.7. Referents within the Elements

Element	First referent	Second referent
	R1	R2
A	Student (s)	Progress
B	Individuals and groups	Work
C	Manner of communicating	Maturity level of child
D	Curriculum	Students
E	Self (student)	Motivation
F	Experiences and resources	Range

For these elements, the referents contained within the various elements are shown in Table 2.7. All elements, except F, contain a reference to students. Therefore, elements A to E can be linked, explicitly, through their reference to students. They each describe conditions supportive of a student-centred approach to teaching and learning. In referring to groups as well as to individuals, and by suggesting equal individual and group work, element B specified a condition only partly supportive of a student-centred approach. In this case it would be expected that elements A, C, D and E would correlate strongly as they can be explicitly co-referenced to one another. Element B would be expected to correlate less strongly with this set of elements.

Element F refers to the provision of a wide range of resources and experiences. As resources and experiences are not referred to in any other elements, element F does not refer directly to any other elements. If, however, the element correlation matrix score indicated a high correlation between elements F and A, for example, then this indicates that the relationship between elements A and F must be implicit; that is, implied by the participant in completing the grid.

Hence a study of the referents of the elements of the repertory grid, with reference to the correlation matrix of the elements, may be used to establish the extent to which the elements co-refer explicitly to one another, and the extent to which relationships between them are perceived by the author of the grid to be implicit. For each repertory grid developed by a teacher participating in the teacher development program, an analysis of the referents of the elements can be used to assess the extent of explicit co-referencing of the elements, and to determine the extent to

Table 2.8. Correlation Matrix for Bipolar Statements

Statements	C1	C2	C3	C4	C5	C6
C1		5	3	3	3	5
C2			2	2	4	4
C3				6	2	4
C4					2	4
C5						2
C6						

which relationships between the various elements are perceived as being implicit.

Correlation of Constructs

Plausibility of the description of effective teaching and learning. For a particular repertory grid, the set of elements gives a description of effective teaching and learning. The triad method is used to elicit bipolar statements, which reflect the similarities and differences between the various elements. This set of bipolar statements forms a framework for interpreting the given description of effective teaching and learning.

The correlation of the bipolar statements can be considered in a similar way to that of the elements. For the above example, the correlation matrix shown in Table 2.8 was derived. In this case C3 and C4 have a correlation score of six. Thus the pattern of matching all the elements with the various poles of the bipolar statements is identical for C3 and C4. If all statements had a correlation score of six for all cases, then the pattern of matching all the elements with the poles of the bipolar statements would be identical. That is, the elements would be matched with one set of polar statements, with one statement being selected from each pair of bipolar statements. In this case this set of statements would form a clear interpretation, in terms of the focus class, of the given description of effective teaching and learning. Under these circumstances this description may be said to be highly plausible in that it can be clearly interpreted by the participant in terms of their focus class.

If the correlation score for two sets of bipolar statements is zero, then this indicates that if the poles of one of these statements were reversed, the correlation score would then be a maximum. Thus a low correlation score indicates a high correlation between the initial pole of one bipolar statement and the emergent pole of the other, or vice versa. Both high and low scores indicate a high correlation, whereas scores intermediate within the range of possible scores show a low correlation.

As above, high and low correlations are an indication of the plausibility of the description of effective teaching and learning in terms of the interpretational framework provided by the set of bipolar statements of the repertory grid.

Analysis and Interpretation of Repertory Grids

For the teacher development program, each teacher completed three repertory grids describing effective teaching and learning as this applied to their focus class. For each of these grids, each teacher considered correlation matrices for both the elements and constructs of the grid, and wrote a detailed interpretation of each grid based on these matrices.

An analysis of the referents of the elements was used to establish the extent of explicit co-referencing between the elements of the grid. When used in conjunction with the correlation matrix of the elements, the analysis of co-reference indicated which elements are seen as implicitly related to one another in the grid. Hence for each completed repertory grid the following information was available:

1 a list of elements;
2 a list of bipolar statements (constructs);
3 a completed repertory grid;
4 correlation matrices for both elements and constructs;
5 the teacher's analysis and interpretation of (1) to (4).

This information was used to examine the co-referencing of elements, their consistency in terms of their correlation with one another, and their plausibility in terms of the correlation of the constructs. This examination led to a discussion of the intelligibility of the description of effective teaching and learning provided by the elements of the grid. A comparison of the three grids completed throughout the teacher development program facilitates the monitoring and assessing of changes in the coherency and plausibility, and hence intelligibility, of the descriptions of effective teaching and learning.

Developing a Theoretical and Procedural Basis for the Teacher Development Program

Applying a Touchstone Approach

The planning and conduct of the teacher development program involve:

i   finding and establishing procedures for the conduct of the program;
ii   developing a suitable reading program;
iii   monitoring and assessing changes in the intelligibility of descriptions of teaching and learning;
iv   evaluating the program.

In Chapter 1 a touchstone approach to theory development was discussed. These discussions had implications for the solution of each of the above phases of the teacher development program. In Chapter 2 Kelly's (1955) theory of personal constructs and its implications for the conduct of the teacher development program have been discussed.

In summary, for the touchstone approach, the conduct of the program involves the following phases for all participants: the describing phase; the recognizing phase; the exploring phase; the sharing phase; the negotiating phase; the reviewing and revising phase. These phases are also implied by the analysis of the implications of Kelly's theory of personal constructs undertaken in this chapter. Thus both theoretical perspectives support the conduct of the program according to the above phases. These phases are used throughout the conduct of the teacher development program.

Theoretical and Procedural Basis of the Teacher Development Program

The theoretical basis for this study is derived from the application of a touchstone approach to theory development and from the corollaries of Kelly's (1955) theory of personal constructs. The procedural basis has been derived from this theoretical basis by considering the implication of the latter for the conduct of, reading content for, monitoring and evaluation of a teacher development program focused on the problem of describing effective teaching and learning for a focus class. These procedures are applied to the conduct of the program as described in Chapter 4;

the reading content of the program as described in Chapter 3; the monitoring and assessment of changes in the intelligibility of participants' descriptions of teaching and learning as described in Chapter 6; and the evaluation of the program as an approach to teacher development as described in Chapter 5.

Chapter 3

Exploring Personal Theories of Teaching

If we assume Kelly's theory of personal constructs as indicating the way teachers construct meaning when considering effective teaching and learning, teacher development programs should encourage such construction. That is, we should encourage teachers to think about and describe effective teaching and learning in terms of bipolar constructs. One way of encouraging this is to emphasize possible bipolar constructs in any reading that the teachers may be required to do in the program. This may enhance the teachers' capacities to describe effective teaching and learning.

Underlying such descriptions are educational assumptions about how students learn, the nature of the knowledge it is most worthwhile for the students to learn, the nature of the society we may wish to encourage through education and, indeed, what it is to be human, the nature of personhood. These assumptions form part of the implied beliefs teachers have about educating and, in particular, about effective teaching and learning. They represent teachers' personal theories of teaching. In the teacher development program described in this book the participating teachers were encouraged to explore and revise their personal theories of teaching using a touchstone approach. The exploration and revision were encouraged by using readings developed to highlight educational issues and problems in terms of bipolar constructs.

This chapter describes and illustrates the development of the content of the reading units for the teacher development program. These units included consideration of a range of approaches to curriculum planning and development, some philosophical issues which underlie these approaches, and some of the implications of these issues for effective teaching and learning. The approaches were selected on the grounds that each has, at some recent stage, been central to debates concerning curriculum planning and development, and that this range of approaches gives an adequate coverage of such discussions.

It was not suggested that such approaches are separate and discrete from one another. Each approach indicated an emphasis on a particular concept in curriculum planning and development. Recently, for example, the concept of objectives appears to have been de-emphasized in favour of the concept of process, and the concept of negotiation has emerged as a key notion in curriculum planning and development. Such emphases do not deny the conceptually eclectic nature of curriculum planning and development. The following approaches were selected:

i   curriculum development and liberal education;
ii   curriculum development and knowledge;
iii curriculum development and objectives;
iv   curriculum development and student abilities;
v   curriculum development and student-centredness;
vi   curriculum development and educational processes;
vii curriculum development and educational discourse;
viii curriculum development and integration.

For each of these approaches, a reading unit was prepared. Each reading was considered by each teacher in the teacher development program. Their totality formed the reading content for the program.

Each of the readings was developed from a survey of recent pertinent literature relating to each approach. From these surveys a précis of some of the philosophical issues which underlie each of these approaches was prepared. This précis was written to highlight these philosophical issues and, in particular, to facilitate their statement as pairs of dichotomous (bipolar) statements. These issues were critical to discussions concerning the educational justification of these various approaches to curriculum planning and development, and included, for example, those issues implied by the objective/relative dichotomy, as this relates to the nature of knowledge.

As each teacher studied each of these readings, they were asked to identify, first, the philosophical issues discussed in each reading. Once these had been identified for a particular approach, each teacher was asked to state each philosophical issue as a pair of dichotomous, or bipolar, statements. For instance, the course unit which discusses curriculum development and knowledge may highlight debates concerning the intrinsic or extrinsic nature of intellectual development. This philosophical issue was stated by the teacher as a pair of bipolar statements. All such issues were then stated as pairs of bipolar statements, or dichotomies.

Each dichotomy was considered in relation to the course participant's focus class. Each teacher was asked to state the implications of each statement of the various dichotomies in general, and then specifically for their focus class. In this way they were required to reflect, initially, on the practical implications for effective teaching and learning of each of the identified dichotomies. Each of the approaches to curriculum development listed above was considered in this way.

The reading content of the teacher development program was divided into four modules of study. These modules, and their subsections, were as follows:

Module A: *Contrasting views of learning and teaching*
   A1: Morgan's (1975) epistemological and psychometric models of the learner
Module B: *Curriculum development and knowledge*
   B1: Curricula and liberal education
   B2: P.H. Hirst's (1974) forms of knowledge
   B3: Intellectual development and forms of knowledge
   B4: Objectivity, truth and inter-subjective agreement
   B5: 'Knowing how' and 'knowing that'
   B6: Polanyi, objectivism and tacit integration
   B7: Summary of issues identified
Module C: *Approaches to curriculum development*
   C1: Curriculum development and objectives
   C2: Curriculum development and student abilities
   C3: Curriculum development and student-centredness
   C4: Curriculum development and educational processes
   C5: Curriculum development and conversation in education
   C6: Curriculum development and integration
   C7: Summary of issues identified
Module D: *Contrasting perspectives of teaching and learning*

The emphasis in developing these readings was to identify, and not resolve, some pertinent philosophical issues. Moreover, it was not suggested that these issues were either necessarily, or practically, resolvable. The view was taken that, in practice, teachers and learners adopt positions which are intermediate to the extreme of positions through which these issues are usually represented. For example, neither a totally objectivist nor a totally relativist position in relation to knowledge was usually adopted.

In the preparation of these readings the implications identified previously in relation to the reading content of the teacher development program were taken into account. In particular, a wide range of approaches to curriculum development was considered. Within the reading for each of these approaches, several different educational perspectives were considered. By relating these perspectives, where possible, to effective teaching and learning, and by referring to the focus classes of the participants, a wide range of plausible, alternative educational perspectives was provided. These perspectives formed a basis for the participants' descriptions of effective teaching and learning, and for their eliciting an extensive range of bipolar constructs.

By the presentation of a wide range of educational perspectives, with balanced emphasis on each, an attempt was made to write all readings in an unbiased, open-minded and intellectually critical style. This approach was supported by the provision of a range of bipolar statements, drawn from each particular reading, at the conclusion of that reading. To illustrate the development of these reading units, units A, B1, B2, C1, C2 and D only have been included.

Reading Units

Module A: Contrasting Views of Learning and Teaching

Much current educational debate concerns the fundamental differences which underlie the views of learning held by teachers and educators. Many would argue that a major difficulty is that, at any time, issues in education have tended to be dominated by one view of learning. In addition, as any proposals with respect to approaches to teaching seem to be closely linked to a particular view of learning, a particular teaching style may predominate. Moreover, the model of the learner may strongly influence not only curriculum content but also assessment and evaluation. Discussions concerning teaching approaches, and curriculum development and evaluation, must involve considering the underlying model of learning, and hence teaching. Furthermore, 'those involved in education often adopt rigidly opposing positions which mitigate against a more constructive and flexible approach. There is now a growing recognition that alternative models can co-exist and enrich rather than detract from development in education' (Pope and Shaw, 1981: 223, 224).

Education and schooling have been traditionally concerned with the knowledge and values of the culture of the society. Such aspects were to be internalized by the students. Teaching had this internalization as its main aim, and sought to achieve this aim through students imitating adult conduct. In this sense, and perhaps in the extreme, Skinner appears to have seen teachers as architects and builders of student behaviour, using curricula based upon analyses of adult behaviour in certain cultural contexts, which have been selected by the adult community as being desirable for transmission to the young. In these circumstances human behaviour is explained in terms of respondent and operant conditioning. Learning is evaluated in terms of changes in overt performances, rather than in thoughts and feelings. Specifically, learning becomes a change in the probability of response under predetermined constraints of operant conditioning. The student's role as a learner is as a passive receiver of knowledge rather than an active participant in the construction of meaning.

A view of education based upon the student as a passive recipient of a selection of the culture of the society appears to have been dominant in Western educational thought. This perspective has been given strong support by the acceptance by educationalists of some psychological theories, particularly those of cognition and motivation, which stress the passivity of the mind. Such theories include associationism-behaviourism, stimulus–response psychology and contingency theories.

Current educational debate, however, indicates renewed interest in the mind as an 'active processor'. On this basis meaning is constructed through the interaction of man with his environment. The emphasis is on the construction of meaning and the interpretation of one's own experiences. Education should, according to this view, and as proposed in differing senses by such writers as Rousseau and Dewey, be directly related to the interests and needs of the student. Importantly, motivation is to come from the student, rather than from the knowledge imposed on the student. The teacher acts as a guide in assisting the student to reconstruct and reinterpret, in terms of personal relevance and significance, the knowledge presented. This approach to learning seeks to give full recognition to the active involvement of the learner in coming to understand their experience of the world in terms of personally relevant interpretational frameworks.

Morgan's (1975) epistemological and psychometric models of the learner provide a convenient basis for contrasting alternative perspectives of teaching and learning in terms of dichotomous or bipolar statements. These models can be used to make the teachers participating in the teacher development program aware of possible assumptions relating to teaching and learning within, or implied by, their descriptions of effective teaching and learning. The consideration of these models in terms of possible pairs of dichotomous or bipolar statements relating to teaching and learning is used to prepare the program participants for eliciting such pairs of statements through the study of the reading units prepared for each selected approach to curriculum development.

A1: Psychometric and epistemological models of the learner. Two contrasting models of learning, involving the passive recipient and the active participant, and their implications for curriculum development, teaching and motivation, and assessment of student progress are summarized by Kathryn Morgan in Nyberg (1975) as the psychometric and epistemological models of learning.

For the psychometric model:

1 the child is regarded as an object, more particularly, as a deficit system whose passivity is a necessary condition for being initiated into public thought forms;

2 the child is regarded as 'having' intelligence in the sense of a specific property which can be measured by objective tests;

3 the world of knowledge is regarded as composed of pre-existing theoretical forms into which the child must be initiated;

4 the pre-existence of such forms and the possession of such by the educator legitimize a highly didactic form of pedagogy;

5 as a possessor of such theoretical forms, the educator assumes the role of societal surrogate, one of whose main roles is to assess the growing congruence of the child's thought forms with the pre-existing standards;

6 educational development consists of growing rationality as the child moves away from the concreteness of his immediate world towards the increasingly abstract theoretical forms;

7 educational achievement consists in progressing towards increasingly specialized and highly discipline-bound subject-matter and is measured in terms of objective evaluative criteria such as behavioural objectives.

Characteristics of the epistemological model include the following:

1 the child is regarded primarily as a subject, that is, as a being who is actively involved in constructing and arranging his knowledge of the world in terms of personally relevant interpretational schemata;

2 the main property which the child is thought to possess and which is most relevant to the educational setting is the non-quantifiable property of curiosity;

3 following the leads of Piaget and Bruner, the world of knowledge is regarded as composed of thought forms which are in a
  constant process of construction and which are dialectically related to the development of individual subjects interacting with
  socially approved and socially distributed knowledge;

4 emphasizing the constructive aspect of human knowledge and
  placing value on intellectual initiative legitimizes a pedagogy
  which is highly interaction oriented;

5 as a similarly constructive, growing subject, the educator assumes
  the role of social model in the process of knowledge construction,
  one of the main responsibilities of which is the heuristic channeling of the pre-existing curiousity of each individual student;

6 successful pedagogy consists not in the measuring of the achievement level of the students but in the ability of the teacher to
  apprehend and recreate the intentionality and subjective reality of
  the students so as to provide greater individual stimulation;

7 although educational achievement is measured in distance from
  starting point to present level of development, this is a highly
  individualized measure. The child is essentially treated as a self-
  regulative being insofar as he controls the sequence and pace of
  experience. In many cases he controls the content of the experience as well, insofar as his interests and desires are often the
  crucial curriculum determinants in the setting. As such, evaluation will be more diffuse, non-quantifiable, highly subjective, and
  more holistic in tone since all dimensions of the student's subjectivity are regarded as worthy of concern in the educational
  setting. (Nyberg, 1975: 125–8)

According to these models, the child may be regarded either as
object or as subject. This raises the question of 'objectivism' being applied
to human beings. An emphasis on objectivism leads to consideration of
human beings in terms of their properties as objects. Research into
human learning, for example, then concentrates on identifying properties
or characteristics of individuals, which are generally associated with what
is regarded, in the context of this study, as effective learning. One such
property is intelligence. This property is to be measured using objective
tests; that is, tests which have universal validity, ideally.

Choosing to describe human learning in terms of the objective properties of the learner leads easily to the quantification of these properties.
This, in turn, lends itself to the notions of surplus and deficiency with
respect to these properties. Hence an apparent incapacity to learn is
described and explained in terms of deficiency of objective properties of

the learner. In Morgan's (1975) terms, the learner is regarded as a deficit system.

If, however, the learner is regarded primarily as a subject, as being actively involved in constructing knowledge and personally relevant interpretations, then the emphasis in describing and explaining human learning will be on the personal qualities of the individual as displayed in particular contexts. That is, no attempt will be made to isolate universally valid qualities or properties, such as intelligence, through which human learning can be understood. In this case intelligence is a qualifier of the particular individual action in a specific context. The learner will be said to have acted intelligently in this particular context, this statement not necessarily having any implications for other situations.

The emphasis on the subjectivity of the individual implies that the learner is active, whilst an emphasis on the learner as an object, and hence as a deficit system, implies passivity. These, and other, fundamentally different perspectives of the learner arise through differing emphases on objectivism and subjectivism. Thus the basic philosophical issue of the balance between objectivism and subjectivism has critical implications for a teacher's perspectives of the learner.

In the psychometric model the student is to be initiated into public thought forms. This implies that the process of learning is one of initiation, which appears to legitimize a form of teaching which has as its overriding purpose this initiation. Thus student interest and needs may well be disregarded on the grounds that the only necessary criterion of successful teaching is completion of the initiation. The means of teaching, and of learning, may be totally subordinated to the end of initiation.

Again, this initiation is to be into pre-existing public thought forms; that is, into bodies of knowledge which are objective in the sense of being public, and hence removed from any variation through individual interpretations, and pre-existing in the sense of being independent of prevailing social and cultural interpretations. This contrasts with the epistemological model, in which the concern is for the construction by the learner of personally relevant frames of reference adapted to the needs and interests of the learner in the particular social and cultural context in which they find themselves at any particular time. The philosophical issue of epistemological objectivism and relativism relates, directly, to these contrasting views of the learner and learning. The former approach implies learning to be the acquisition, by initiation, of objective knowledge, whilst the latter implies the construction of personal understanding, and hence of socially and culturally relevant knowledge.

For the psychometric model, the teacher is required to possess the theoretical thought forms, or bodies of objective knowledge, and to act in such a way that the learner's thought forms grow increasingly congruent with them. The extent of this congruence is assessed by the teacher in terms of standards intrinsic to these bodies of knowledge. The emphasis of the psychometric model on objectivism, objective knowledge, initiation and congruence with pre-existing standards legitimizes a highly didactic form of teaching. On the other hand, the emphasis in the epistemological model on subjectivism, personal interpretation within socially approved and distributed knowledge construction and the heuristic channeling of pre-existing curiousity tends to legitimize a highly interaction oriented style of teaching which values individual initiative.

For the psychometric model, educational development is assessed in terms of the student's rationality as indicated by a capacity to reproduce, at ever-increasing levels of abstraction, public thought forms. In so doing, the student progresses away from knowledge of the concreteness of his immediate surroundings to the privacy of increasingly abstract thought forms. This progress is assessed in terms of the pre-existing and public standards of each of the thought forms. That is, educational development proceeds according to, and is assessed in terms of, public and external norms and criteria. In contrast, student development, as indicated by the epistemological model, is not referenced to external norms and criteria, but proceeds according to the channeling of the non-quantifiable, and pre-existing, property of the student, namely curiosity. Development occurs according to individual stimulation.

The two models represent contrasting perspectives of educational development, the psychometric model representing development in terms of external norms pre-existing within public bodies of knowledge, and the epistemological model portraying development in terms of the norms of the individual, as these come into play in the individual, on the basis of pre-existing curiosity, seeking personally relevant interpretations of their experience. The issue of internal and external referencing of educational development will be discussed later in this reading program.

For the psychometric model, achievement is progressing towards increasingly specialized and highly discipline-bound subject-matter. Educational achievement is measured in terms of objective criteria, such as behavioural objectives. That is, the assessment of educational achievement for this model is through an emphasis on objectivism. Assessment of achievement for the epistemological model, on the other hand, stresses subjectivism. Considering the notion of educational achievement for these models raises the issue of objectivism and subjectivism.

Finally, the approach to assessment and evaluation for the psychometric model is through the progressive development of more highly specialized, abstract, quantifiable and objective criteria. That is, it proceeds according to a reductionist approach. Evaluation for the epistemological model is more diffuse, non-quantifiable, highly subjective and more holistic.

Module B: Curriculum Development and Knowledge

This section is concerned with those approaches to curriculum planning which have as their central feature the selection of knowledge; that is, those approaches based on selecting that knowledge which is most worthwhile for inclusion in a curriculum. The educational justification of the selection of particular knowledge and the rejection of other knowledge has usually been based on arguments concerning either the intrinsic worth of some knowledge or its utilitarian value.

Each of these arguments is examined in this section. This examination begins with a critical discussion of the development of the concept of liberal education. This leads to a consideration of the relationship of the nature of knowledge to the concept of liberal education, and hence to a discussion of Hirst's proposals with respect to forms of knowledge, and their implications for curriculum development. On these bases some of the philosophical issues central to the above approaches to curriculum development are identified and discussed.

B1: Curricula and liberal education. Prior to the conclusion of the War of Independence in 1776, the traditions of a liberal education, as they had developed in England, were shared by both England and America. The class structure, which characterized English society at this time, appeared to rest upon hierarchical assumptions based on heredity. These assumptions, and the consequent social structure, remained substantially unchanged in England. However, the unsettling political and social ideas, which were imported to America and which found expression in newly won independence, had a marked effect on the underlying assumptions and values of American society.

In England the regulative effect of the social class structure remained. As a consequence, curricula tended to cater for the particular needs of the various social classes and to reaffirm these needs. Although political representation was formalized, this representation remained 'virtual' in the sense that 'representation has nothing to do with obeying popular wishes, but means the enactment of the national good by a select elite' (Pitkin, 1967: 170). Questions of the relationship of education to the social structure of society did not arise, and the relationship of such questions to political and social leadership was not considered to be of importance. Debate on curricula, strongly influenced by the traditions of Oxford and Cambridge universities, was mainly concerned with curriculum content and the place of the classics and the sciences in a liberal education. Discussions on liberal education were about the education of the upper classes and, as observed by Newman, 'Its object is nothing more than intellectual excellence.... Knowledge is one thing, virtue another' (Kerr, 1976: 110–11). In supporting this view, Reid states: 'The social and institutional forces of the time prevented controversies about man and society and directed them into discussions of what content best trained the mind for "intellectual excellence"' (Reid, 1980: 254).

Furthermore, each period of identifiable social change seems to have embodied a reinterpretation of liberal education in terms of its social and political mores. In Georgian England, for example, 'it was given the immense burden of rendering men and women sociable, tolerant and broad-minded in situations where also every encouragement was given to the pursuit of personal advantage' (Rothblatt, 1976: 102). On the other hand, in Victorian England, and within the context of industrialism, liberal education was directed towards problems within this society and those who could provide speculative solutions, which gave the often turbulent society a sense of direction and purpose. During the nineteenth century the great universities, through the churches, became the dominant institutional bases of liberal education. Liberal education thus ceased to be personally defined in terms of such things as books, travel and works of art, and became tied to institutions.

The study of the development of an alternative notion of liberal education in America may be assisted by considering the evolution of the major universities in that country. Whilst these may have been concerned, initially, with the development of practical skills, they were also concerned with 'a reconstruction of institutionalized cognitive activities, creating a structure oriented towards discovery growth, inquiry: "research"' (Wegener, 1978: 57). Moreover, and in contrast to institutions in England, those in America were to incorporate the ideas of a political democracy. Educational institutions would be open to all, and would be directed towards the benefit of all members of society. This is not to devalue, necessarily, intellectual excellence, for 'it becomes expedient for promoting the public happiness that those persons whom nature had endowed with genius and virtue, should be rendered by liberal education worthy to receive and able to guard the sacred deposit of rights and liberties of their fellow citizens' (Reid, 1980: 257). Curriculum decisions were to be made within the principles and procedures of a political democracy, and to be justified on a utilitarian basis. That is, curriculum decisions were substantially based within the socio-political context.

Thus two perspectives of liberal education emerged — the one based upon intellectual excellence developed through the acquisition of knowledge and understanding, and the other on principles determined within the socio-political context. Rothblatt (1976) suggests that the debate on the nature of liberal education, as suggested by these differing perspectives, focuses on three central issues, each of which gives rise to necessarily ambiguous arguments. These are:

i   differences which stem from the arts and the sciences;
ii differences arising from the relationships of arts and sciences to religion and politics; and
iii difficulties about the old and new in knowledge most worth having.

The management of liberal education is concerned, therefore, with the management of differences arising from decisions made about the curriculum for liberal education. That is, questions relating to curriculum decisions for liberal education are not logically resolvable. Liberal education is an ideal and, as such, is characterized by unresolved differences, and hence cannot assume any permanent embodiment. Rothblatt sees the central problem of liberal education as 'the relation of reason and argument to social values and alternative realities' (1976: 176).

For Hirst (1974), liberal education is defined as the pursuit of unalterable realities to which education must address itself through the study of the forms of knowledge as discussed in *Knowledge and the Curriculum* (1974). In contrast, Schwab (1969) suggests that the essence of liberal education is 'the management of an inherently ambiguous idea in the interest of shaping engaged moral agents' (Reid, 1980: 253). (Note: Students participating in the program will have previously read 'Liberal Education and the Nature of Knowledge', Hirst (1974).)

For Hirst (1974), moral action is to be based on the knowledge gained through initiation into that form of knowledge, moral knowledge. For Schwab, moral actions are shaped through knowledge gained by participating in attempts to resolve the inherent ambiguities of a liberal education. In the first instance, coming to know how to act morally means being able to reason and argue axiomatically within the form of knowledge. For Schwab, coming to know is the progressive development of alternative realities through social interaction, with each such reality being characterized by rules and norms of moral action.

Attempts to recognize these two differing perspectives within school curricula, that is, to retain intellectual excellence as an aim whilst paying due attention to social and political aims, such as equipping students for their participation in a democratic society, may highlight the need to find ways of accommodating the philosophical differences underlying these perspectives within an educational rationale for curricula. Some such differences are identified in the remainder of these readings. The philosophical assumptions underlying these differences are then expressed as dichotomies, or bipolar statements.

B2: P.H. Hirst's forms of knowledge. P.H. Hirst's views on the nature of liberal education and its epistemological basis are substantially contained in *Knowledge and the Curriculum* (1974). The seminal essay within this collection is 'Liberal Education and the Nature of Knowledge', which was first published in *Philosophical Analysis and Education* (1965), edited by R. Archambault. Throughout this paper Hirst is concerned with providing an adequate characterization and justification of liberal education. The search for a definition of such an education is, according to Hirst, justified on the basis that to deny the value of such a search would be to bring into question the worthiness of the pursuit of rational knowledge and '... to question the pursuit of any kind of rational knowledge is in the end self-defeating, for the questioning itself depends upon the very principles whose use is finally called into question' (Archambault, 1965: 113). Education is to be centrally concerned with developing the pupil's knowledge, rationality or intellect.

Hirst (1974) appears to have misgivings about the absolute nature of his proposal when he states that, with respect to liberal education and its dependence on the forms of knowledge, it

> ... is simply about the present state of affairs but that state of affairs is not to be regarded as either a transient articulation of a merely socially relative concept of knowledge, or the latest expression of an absolute and invariant framework implicit in knowledge (Hirst, 1974: 95–6).

For Hirst, 'the logically most fundamental objectives of all are those of the cognitive kind, on the basis of which, out of which, or in relation to which, all others must be developed' (Hirst and Peters, 1970: 62). Liberal education is based on 'the nature and significance of knowledge itself' and 'ever since the Greeks has been repeatedly located in man's conception of the diverse Forms of Knowledge he had achieved' (Hirst, 1974: 32).

For the Greeks, the development of the concept of liberal education was dependent on the significance of the acquisition of knowledge to the development of the mind, and the relationship of this knowledge to reality. Knowledge was significant in that its pursuit was essential to the ultimate development of the mind. It was asserted that through the 'right' use of reason 'the mind comes to know the essential nature of things, and can apprehend what is real and immutable' (Hirst, 1974: 31). Thus knowledge can be progressively attained, and will be incorporated into a comprehensive hierarchical structure, the pattern of which is formed as knowledge of reality is developed. Education is based, therefore, upon a metaphysical conception of knowledge. This view is justified in that not only is it based upon what is true, and is such that it has value to the individual in the development of mind, but also in that it is essential to man's understanding of how he ought to live. Thus, for the Greeks, the significance of the concept of liberal education arose from the position given to knowledge in basic metaphysical doctrines for unifying the concepts of mind and reality.

Both the definition and the justification of Hirst's concept of a liberal education are dependent upon his thesis that knowledge is structured into forms. 'By these is meant, of course, not collections of information, but the complex ways of understanding experience, which man has achieved, which are publicly specifiable, and which are gained through learning' (Hirst, 1974: 35). It is maintained that, by the sharing of conceptual schema and their associated public symbols, such an understanding becomes possible and acquires objectivity in the sense that there is public consensus as to the meaning of symbols. That is, the objective expression of assertions relating to experience in terms of these symbols permits the development of public criteria against which the truth or validity of such assertions may be assessed. Continued and progressive assessments enable the probing and (public) description of more complex experiences, and thus the further development of knowledge. Hirst contends that it is only in terms of the symbols detailing the structure of such knowledge that emotional experiences or mental attitudes and beliefs become intelligible. Thus to acquire knowledge is to become aware of experience as being structured and organized, and made meaningful in a specific way. This structure does not, Hirst considers, arise because the mind has predetermined patterns of functioning — to have a mind is to have experience according to conceptual frameworks.

Each developed form of knowledge is characterized by the following related distinguishing features.

1   They involve certain central concepts that are peculiar in character to the form. For example, those of gravity, acceleration, hydrogen and photosynthesis characteristic of the sciences; num-

ber, integral and matrix in mathematics; God, sin and predestination in religion; ought, good and wrong in moral knowledge.

2 In a given form of knowledge these and other concepts that denote, if perhaps in a very complex way, certain aspects of experience, form a network of possible relationship in which experience can be understood. As a result the form has a distinctive logical structure. For example, the terms and statements of mechanics can be meaningfully related in certain strictly limited ways only, and the same is true of historical explanation.

3 The form, by virtue of its particular terms and logic, has expressions or statements (possibly answering a distinctive type of question) that in some way or other, however indirect it may be, are testable against experience. This is the case in scientific knowledge, moral knowledge, and in the arts; no questions are explicit and the criteria for the tests are only partially expressible in words. Each form, then, has distinctive expressions that are testable against experience in accordance with particular criteria that are peculiar to the form.

4 The forms have developed particular techniques and skills for exploring experience and testing their distinctive expressions, for instance the techniques of the sciences and those of the various literary arts. The result has been the amassing of all the symbolically expressed knowledge that we now have in the arts and the sciences. (Hirst, 1974: 44)

Thus it is proposed that the domain of human knowledge can be differentiated into a number of logically distinct 'forms', none of which is ultimately reducible in character to the others. On the basis of these characteristics it is proposed that there are the following distinct disciplines or forms of knowledge: mathematics, physical sciences, human sciences, history, religion, literature and the fine arts, and philosophy.

'Structure of knowledge' theories, such as that proposed by Hirst, are characterized by arguments that knowledge is structured into broad fields or categories called, for example, disciplines, communities of discourse, forms of knowledge, or realms of meaning. Such theories propose that conceptual structures are necessarily the prime determinants of an intellectual education. Gardner (1972) has suggested a 'structure-of-knowledge' theory on the basis of a need to provide a theory of education which is value-free, unified, consistent and non-realist. It is further proposed that there is a link between structured knowledge and education. This relationship may take one of two forms:

    i   knowledge is structured through communication and hence is available for learning;

    ii to think is to use conceptual structures, i.e. there is a logical relationship between the conceptual structure of the knowledge and the understanding of it.

Hirst (1974) proposes that the conceptual structures to be used in the development of rational thought are those which are characteristic of the forms of knowledge. Consequently, the forms of knowledge are to be the basis of intellectual education.

According to 'structure of knowledge' theories, a discipline has an internal structure of key concepts (substantive structure) and rules of inference and truth criteria (syntactic structure). These structures are used in rational thought. Disciplines may sometimes be grouped together on the basis of similarity of internal structures, e.g. physical sciences. The content of the curriculum should exemplify, and illuminate, these structures.

An important consequence of such theories is that there are no principles of thought, or truth criteria, to be found outside these disciplines, against which the validity of these proposals could be judged. That is, there are no transdisciplinary criteria for truth. This difficulty usually gives rise to either a transcendental argument, such as that proposed by Hirst with respect to rational man, or to the proposal of metaphysical principles, as for Plato and the theory of forms. The major difficulty of a 'structure-of-knowledge' theory occurs when the move is made from the description of the structures to a recommendation for curriculum selection. For those who support such a theory, the claim is that the key concepts, truth criteria and rules of inference of the disciplines are necessary and sufficient for the development of a rational mind. From this claim at least the following key questions arise:

    i   What is meant by necessary?

    ii If one uses structures of knowledge, other than those found in the disciplines, is one non–rational?

    iii What is meant by sufficient? Do we only need the disciplines for rational thought?

    iv Do the disciplines represent a structure within language and social convention, or structures within the world of experience? Or are the disciplines the product of innate structures of the mind which are common to human beings? That is, do the structures of the disciplines have the status of Kantian categories and are they, therefore, preconditions for objective thought?

The range of alternatives for the structures of the disciplines includes:

   i   that they are culturally relative;
   ii that they are conventional, as in language or tradition;
  iii that they are correct and 'in the world';
  iv that they are correct and 'in the mind'.

If they are 'in the mind', they are either predispositions for objective thought or logical prerequisites for objective thought. Thus 'structure' must be conventional or 'in the world' or 'in the mind'.

If the structures are to be outside our introspective or reflective experiences, it must be asked how we are able to gain access to such structures. Is this world of external experience structured in such a way as to form the basis for the structure of disciplines? Walkling (1979) indicates the logical impossibility of answering these questions by reference to an external world. As Hume wrote, '"it is in vain to ask, whether there be body or not" since the questioner "cannot defend his reason by reason". That is, we cannot even temporarily suspend the conceptual framework in which we have minds, to see whether the world is as that framework makes it seem' (Walkling, 1979: 65). The question of the logical necessity of the structures of the disciplines cannot, on this basis, be settled by referring to an external reality.

As suggested previously, if the structures of knowledge are to be intrinsic to the mind, then they may either by psychological predispositions or logical prerequisites for objective thought. That is, either human beings have in common an innate set of predispositions which structures thought and experience and hence knowledge, or having objective experience at all may mean that there are particular logical constraints on the possible arrangement of ideas and hence of knowledge. In both cases such innate capacities would be logically prior to experience.

Any discussion of the possibility and necessity of such capacities must take place in terms of their public symbolism, either as language or other symbol systems. But any innate structuring capacity, which may be manifested as a predisposition to learn a particular language, for example, is not evidence of similar capacities for other symbol systems. Evidence for a predisposition with respect to language or mathematics is not evidence for the belief that a similar capacity exists for the natural sciences.

'Structure-of-knowledge' theorists appear to be arguing that, in the first instance, it is the apparent temporal permanence of the regularity of the experienced world which persuades us that it exists outside consciousness. To be 'rational' is to be aware of, and take into account in terms of behaviour, the constancy and regularity of the experienced world. Rational knowledge of this world must be given in terms of its structures. That is, there is a relationship between the structure of knowledge and the structure of the experienced world or reality. The form of this relationship will depend upon the view taken of reality. Four possibilities seem to be suggested.

First, it may be proposed that there is a world external to our consciousness to which we have access, and that the structures of the disciplines directly represent the structures of this 'real' world. That is, knowledge is to be viewed objectively as a unique representation of the 'real' world, being independent of, and abstract from, the observer, and invariant in time. Alternatively, it could be argued that, as before, there is an external world to which we have access, but that the structures of the disciplines are conventions. Such conventions have the effect of making the world appear coherent, but such appearances, and hence conventions, are socially constructed and culturally determined. This is to express a relativist view of knowledge. Third, it may be proposed that we only have access to our personal impressions. In this case the structure of the disciplines must, as previously discussed, arise either from innate structures of the mind or from the logic of experiencing. The structures of the disciplines are then the public ways of making these impressions coherent. Finally, we may only have access to our impressions, and the structures of the disciplines are conventions through which our impressions assume regularity.

This section raises the following issues:

i   epistemological objectivism and relativism;
ii the fundamental basis of the perceived regularity and coherence of experience — is the basis for this regularity in the mind, in experience, in our impressions, or in a common and shared external reality?

Hence the critical philosophical questions raised in this section are:

i   Is knowledge absolute and objective, or socially constructed and culturally determined, that is, relative?
ii Are the structures of the disciplines
    — culturally relative;
    — conventional as in language, or tradition;
    — in an external world;
    — in the mind?

Each of these questions can be expressed in terms of a contrasting philosophical position. These positions may be stated as pairs of bipolar statements, or dichotomies, including: Knowledge is transcultural./ Knowledge is culturally relative. Knowledge is not socially constructed, i.e. objective./ Knowledge is socially constructed, i.e. subjective. The structures of the disciplines are culturally relative./ The structures of the disciplines are acultural. The structures of the disciplines are conventional, as in language./ The structures of the disciplines are not in the conventions of language. The structures of the disciplines are traditional./ The structures of the disciplines are non-traditional. The structures of the disciplines correspond to structures in the experienced world./ The structures of the disciplines correspond to structures in the mind.

Module C: Approaches to Curriculum Development

C1: Curriculum development and objectives. During the 1950s and 1960s a new enthusiasm developed for the precision and specificity apparently offered by the planning of curricula in terms of educational objectives. This development was perhaps led by an upsurge in interest in the application of analytic philosophy to the analysis of educational concepts in the United Kingdom, and paralleled in the United States of America by the increasing influence of Bloom *et al.* (1956) and by the acceptance of objectives-based procedures of accountability, such as management by objectives. In Britain the work of Hirst and Peters, in particular, and in America that of Bloom and his co-workers may be seen as important in legitimizing an objectives movement in education and in curriculum development. This movement had its beginning with the work of Taba (1962). Curriculum planning was to proceed on the basis that the educational purposes of the curriculum would be translated, initially, into sets of objectives.

Kelly (1982) lists four main arguments for the acceptance of the objectives approach to curriculum planning. The most persuasive arguments are logical, educational, politico-economic and scientific. For any activity to be considered rational (logical), it is argued that its goals and purposes must be clearly formulable; to educate 'rationally' requires the clear formulation of purposes, and their subsequent translation into objectives. This formulation will assist the evaluation of achievement. Evaluation will be necessary as a basis for public accountability. Thus public accountability is supported by the 'rationality' of the objective approach to curriculum planning.

The development of the notion of rational planning was accompanied by an upsurge in technological development, particularly as this related to space technology. A consequent re-emphasis on the priorities given to the natural sciences in curricula meant that many of the most comprehensive and objectives-based curriculum developments occurred in physics, chemistry, biology and the earth sciences. Hence the objectives movement acquired a 'scientific' orientation as measurable, observable and replicable objectives were favoured as, for example, for behavioural objectives.

Because of the apparent high status of science within society, arguments supporting the objectives approach in terms of its perceived scientific validity appear to carry considerable weight. This may reflect a general assumption that the 'scientific' practice of anything is desirable. Associated notions of precision, accuracy, objectivity and rationality support this assumption. However, this approach implicitly contradicts its claim to be value-neutral by unquestioningly applying what are believed to be scientific values to the practice of education.

In the first instance an objective may be thought of as constituting an action, thought or feeling. Consider the objective 'To compute accurately'. This objective specifies the object or purpose 'to compute accurately'. The object of the action to be taken is to compute accurately. This is what is to be understood by the objective 'to compute accurately'. Similarly, objects of thought or feeling may constitute an objective. Thus, by specifying objects of action, thought or feeling, objectives express purposes or intentions. The objectives approach to curriculum development depends upon educational purposes being expressed as objects of action, thought or feeling, that is, as objectives.

This approach has, however, sometimes been associated with objectivism, that is, with a tendency to lay stress on what is objective, or external to the mind, and hence on objective knowledge. This stress on knowledge which is given and non-human may lead to a view that educating is the process of transmitting selections of given knowledge to the student with as little distortion as possible. 'Educated' students are those who can demonstrate that they have received this knowledge in its given form, and have come to know what is 'objectively' true.

Rorty (1980) argues against the notion of objective knowledge. One of his important questions is: 'What is truth?' His belief is that there are two types of answers. The first implies that truth is external, to be searched for and found, whilst the second implies that truth is relative and constructed by humans. He argues that the former conception of truth is the result of the human task being mistakenly formulated as that of representing some world of 'given' regularities, mirroring it as it 'really' is, undistorted by any subjective shaping, such as through the use of value-laden language. The ultimate escape from such shaping is the use of mathematical symbols, for the special character of mathematical truths appears to be that they cannot be misjudged or misreported. The truth in this case is imposed by the objects known. It is a necessary truth. It is this sense of unarguable certainty in mathematical truths which, ever since Plato's epistemology, has been used to divide truth into that which is unquestionable and 'objective' truth and that which is 'made by humans', subjective and non-scientific and, therefore, 'less true' in some way.

However, for Rorty (1980), there are no given regularities, and truth does not result from a clearer representation, or a more faithful mirroring, of something outside the self, but is something we make ourselves. All truths are a matter of victory in argument, and never final or 'necessary'. Our only rational certainty comes from conversation between persons, rather than through interaction within a non-human reality. The type of scientific certainty in question is not only impossible, but also undesirable in that it would lead to closure and the end of all inquiry. Borrowing Oakshott's phrase, Rorty suggests that it is the 'conversation of mankind' which forms the 'ultimate context within which knowledge is to be understood' (1980: 389).

By way of contrast, for Popper (1963), the growth of knowledge progresses through problem solving. Objective reality is defined as 'World 3', a world of 'objective structures which are products, not necessarily intentional, of minds or living creatures, but which, once produced, exist independently of them' (Magee, 1973: 60). Even mathematical theories are still objective in this sense only, being firstly created by human beings, but then becoming autonomous in Popper's World 3. For Popper, all knowledge, all present truth, is the result of subjecting our speculations to initial discussion, and hence the continual interaction between World 3 and World 2, the subjective mind. Learning takes place, not through any discovery by observation of something non-human in the physical world of material things, World 1, but through the interaction of the other two worlds, through intrusion of the past and present theories which make up World 3, those developed by humans as they put their expectations to the test of experience and criticism, and which are, therefore, not objective in any sense of being beyond human control, fixed and unchangeable.

If, so Rorty and Popper suggest, truth is something we construct through human action based on language, then language becomes a tool, which is autonomous in World 3, but does not shape our knowledge or distort 'reality'. The development of self-consciousness and knowledge depends on a wider grasp of the world, an ability to 'connect' temporally, spatially and causally as past, present and future form a continuum in which the present is seen to grow from the past, and the regularities observed in the past are the basis of our expectations and inferences about the probable shape of the future.

Thus attempts to justify educationally the objectives approach to curriculum development, and the association of this approach with the notion of objectivism, lead to the consideration of a range of philosophical issues. As before, each of these issues may be stated in terms of a range of pairs of dichotomous statements, including: All knowledge is relative./ All knowledge is absolute. Truth is external./ Truth is relative to and constructed by humans. Truth mirrors the regularities of experience./ Truth is something we make ourselves. Truth is a matter of victory in argument./ Truth is imposed by the object known.

C2: Curriculum development and student abilities.   As general dissatisfaction with the objectives approach to curriculum development grew, particularly as a result of its apparent inappropriateness for the more expressive areas of the curriculum, process approaches, which focused on the experiences of learning rather than the outcomes of learning, became favoured. This movement towards an emphasis on the process of educating appears to have given renewed currency to the idea of a general education developing general powers of the mind, and of abilities or skills not being confined to particular areas of knowledge or subjects. A central question to any debate on the nature of liberal education is whether or not there are general abilities or powers of the mind. A classic discussion of this question is contained in John Locke's *An Essay Concerning Human Understanding*. As John W. Yolten, the editor of a new edition (1976) of Locke's essay, states:

> The focus of Locke's argument is that all of our ideas have but two sources — sensation and reflection. Sensations give us ideas of external objects and their properties. Reflection gives us ideas of our own mental faculties.

> The better to conceive the ideas we receive from sensation, it may not be amiss for us to consider them in reference to the different ways whereby they make their approaches to our minds and make themselves perceivable to us.

> First, then, there are some which came into our minds by one sense only.

> Secondly, there are others that convey themselves into the mind by more senses than one.

Thirdly, others that are had from reflection only.

Fourthly, there are some that make themselves way and are suggested to the mind by all the ways of sensation and reflection. (Locke, 1976: 47)

Furthermore,

The two great principal actions of the mind, which are most frequently considered, and which are so frequent that everyone that pleases may take notice of them in himself, are these two:

Perception, or Thinking;
or
Volition or Willing.

The power of thinking is called the understanding and the power of volition is called the will, and these two powers of abilities in the mind are denominated faculties. Of some of the modes of these simple ideas of reflection, such as remembrance, discerning, reasoning, judging, knowledge, fault, etc., I shall occasion to speak hereafter. (Locke, 1976: 52)

Thus these powers or abilities require sensations for their functions, but are original in the mind and may be developed through exercise.

But the question may not be concerned with the originality of the general powers of the mind as developed by exercise of the mind. Rather, it may be asked whether or not general powers of the mind can be the outcome of learning. In this case it could be argued that something would have to be presupposed as being original. 'Children must bring something into the world but it need not be general powers of the kind that cut across whole ranges of curricula subjects' (Dearden, 1980: 280).

The resurgence of the popularity of a 'general abilities' (competences, capabilities, and so on) approach to curriculum planning may be due to the proliferation of knowledge, and the possibility of some knowledge becoming obsolescent, and hence the need to ensure that students learn something of more lasting value. The development of general abilities, or general powers of the mind, is seen as offering the possibility of a curriculum outcome of lasting value. This is not a new notion. Newman (1853), in discussing the future development of university education, supported a general powers of the mind thesis. The '. . . aim was culti-vate a faculty of entering with comparative ease into any subject of thought, and of taking up with aptitude any avenue or profession'

(Newman, 1853: Preface). Support for this view is provided by Wegener (1978), who sees liberal education as the cultivation of 'certain critical powers of reflection which can then be employed in many different specific directions' (Wegener, 1978: 27).

Similar arguments have been used, as for Dewey (1916), to support the development of particular general powers through the study of particular subjects. The special task of the study of English literature may be seen as the development of creative imagination, history to develop practical wisdom, and philosophy to develop logical thought. Whilst the development of these or, indeed, any other general abilities or powers of mind may be desirable, the question remains as to whether or not it is even logically, let alone practically, possible.

Attempts may be made to define liberal education in terms of the development of general mental abilities, which are agreed to be educationally desirable. However, the acquisition and/or development of any such abilities can only become apparent through associated publicly describable and testable achievements. Such abilities are specified only in public terms and criteria, and such a specification is dependent upon the public features of the knowledge concerned. If mathematical knowledge is describable in public terms, then those activities assumed to indicate the exercise of a mathematical ability may be described and assessed publicly. Hence, if such public specification is necessary to the indication of mental abilities, then no such specification can occur without a full account of the public features of the related areas of knowledge. For Hirst, therefore, any ability must be exercised on something specific, and judged according to those specific standards of success inherent within, and characteristic of, the forms of knowledge. Abilities are form-specific rather than general.

Griffiths (in Archambault, 1965) argues that mentalistic concepts such as 'intelligence' and 'imagination' must be given public expression in terms of particular activity. Thus the force of the word 'intelligent' will depend entirely on what it actually qualifies. An intelligent mathematician is different, therefore, from an intelligent historian. Such arguments, however, seem to show that specific abilities are necessary, but not that general abilities are impossible.

The key question raised in this section is whether or not student abilities, or powers of the mind, are general or specific. If they are general, they do not require the study of any particular body or form of knowledge, or the completion of specific tasks. If, however, abilities, or powers of the mind, are specific, they can only be developed through the study of particular bodies or forms of knowledge, or by the completion of certain tasks. The key issues raised in this section can be dichotomously expressed in the following pair of statements: Student abilities, or powers of the mind, are specific./ Student abilities, or powers of the mind, are general.

Module D: Contrasting Perspectives of Teaching and Learning

In Module A Morgan (1975), in discussing socialization, social models and the open education movement, proposes that there are two dominant structuring models, the one relating to public schools and the other subjective, and more holistic in tone, since all dimensions of the student's subjectivity are regarded as worthy of concern in the educational setting (1975: 127, 128).

The set of philosophical issues raised within Modules B and C of these readings is also contained in Morgan's epistemological and psychometric models of the learner. That is, these models summarize the philosophical issues identified in Modules B and C in a form which directly relates them to learning and teaching. Both the philosophical issues identified and their implications for teaching and learning are encapsulated in the contrasts which can be drawn between the characteristics of these models. These contrasts may be categorized as follows:

	Perspective A	Perspective B
i	Learning is: initiation, intellectually passive, receiving, public, increasingly abstract, governed by objective properties.	Learning is: creating, intellectually active, constructing, personal, increasingly personal, governed by subjective qualities.
ii	Development is according to: external principles and criteria.	Development is according to: internal principles and criteria.
iii	Achievement is assessed according to: growing congruence, public standards, pre-existing standards, objective standards.	Achievement is assessed according to: growing individuality, personal standards, continually revised standards, subjective standards.

| iv | Knowledge is:
public,
objective,
pre-existing. | Understanding is:
personal
subjective,
continuously being created. |
| v | Teaching is:
didactic. | Teaching is:
interaction oriented. |

These perspectives suggest some bipolar statements, or dichotomies, which may be used in interpreting descriptions of effective teaching and learning, and which arise from the preceding readings.

Chapter 4

Running the Program

The teacher development program was conducted in three periods, each of one week (five days). The program ran for six hours per day. Sixteen senior teachers enrolled in, and completed, the program.

To help focus on describing effective teaching and learning for an actual class, each teacher was asked, prior to the commencement of the teacher development program, to select a focus class. This class was preferably a class, or group of students, the teacher was currently teaching, and was likely to continue to teach for the remainder of the year during which the teacher development program was being conducted.

Having selected this focus class, each teacher described teaching approaches taken to ensure that effective learning takes place in this class. These approaches referred to the total teaching program for the class for the year, and not to any specific part of it. In describing these approaches the teachers considered questions such as:

What are the priorities to be considered when planning to teach this class?

What are the conditions under which students can learn most effectively?

What are the main difficulties, if any, in teaching this class?

What are the characteristics of the students which markedly affect the ways the class is taught?

What are the best teaching strategies for motivating the class?

What parts of the program do you teach most effectively and why?

What parts of the program do the students learn most easily and why?

Each teacher had this information available at the commencement of the program.

Assessment of the work of the teachers in the program was based upon the content of their professional journal. The following instructions for completing the professional journal were given:

As well as the material suggested in the description of the Professional Journal for inclusion in the Journal, each member will be expected to include all working papers and other written materials developed and used during the conduct of the program. In particular, all papers used in repertory grids related to effective teaching and learning must be included. These should include reflective evaluations by each teacher on the work they have completed at the end of the various stages of the program. Opportunities to complete such evaluations will be given during the program. During this program a range of readings will be studied. Two approaches to this study will be suggested. The first involves direct attempts to apply repertory grid techniques to the reading, whilst the second uses a 'key question' approach. Whichever aproach is used to study a particular reading, it is expected that the results of this study will be included in the Professional Journal.

The presentation of the program was based on the following ordered set of activities as described earlier:

describing,
recognizing,
exploring,
sharing,
negotiating,
reviewing and revising.

These activities were used as a basis for organizing and presenting the teacher development program.

Describing

To begin with, each teacher came to the class with a set of statements describing effective teaching and learning, as perceived by them, for their focus class. These preliminary descriptions were made the focus of discussion with the other teachers. For each of the questions listed in the above request, class discussion was used to discuss particular features of effective teaching and learning, which could be considered in formulating answers to these questions. In this way a list of possible answers was developed with the whole class. Each teacher was asked to consider their preliminary description of effective teaching and learning for their focus class, and, in the light of the above discussions, add to, delete, or modify this description as they considered appropriate. (To depersonalize this task, teachers were asked to think in terms of developing a description of effective teaching and learning for a beginning teacher, who had been asked to take over their focus class in the near future.)

Sharing, Negotiating, Reviewing and Revising

The class was then asked to consider the nature of the grouping, which would enhance the sharing of these descriptions of effective teaching and learning. In particular, the class was asked to decide whether or not groupings should be mixed in terms of the teaching backgrounds of the group members such as in infant, primary, secondary and further education, or specialized in that all members with a secondary education background, for example, should be placed in one group. The class unanimously chose the former procedure, emphasizing the need to widen perspectives of effective teaching and learning. The groups were formed on this basis.

Then each class member shared their preliminary descriptions of effecive teaching and learning for their focus class with other members of the group. At this stage no attempt was made to negotiate any agreed description of effective teaching and learning. As a result of this sharing, each class member had the opportunity to review and revise their description. These descriptions were shared with the whole class. During this sharing participants were asked to state their descriptions as a series of grammatically simple sentences, with each sentence dealing with only one feature of effective teaching and learning where possible. Descriptions were then reviewed and revised to meet that requirement.

Expression of the descriptive statements used by class members in terms of the bipolar statements perceived to be implied by them was then demonstrated. For example, the descriptive statement supplied by one teacher was: 'Effective teaching and learning involves the development of self-motivation by providing enjoyable, interesting and purposeful activities.' The teacher perceived this statement as implying two possible alternative descriptions:

A   Effective teaching and learning results from the self-motivation of the students.
B   Effective teaching and learning requires the extrinsic motivation of students.

These statements are referred to as bipolar statements, or dichotomies.

In eliciting such bipolar statements, the class members were encouraged to consider bipolarity in terms of alternative educational perspectives as perceived by them within the current discourse on educational issues. To familiarize students with this procedure, a range of examples of descriptive statements was taken, and the eliciting of bipolar statements demonstrated. Then each class member was asked to use the descriptive statements prepared for their focus class to generate a range of bipolar statements.

Negotiating

Working in the same groups, each group shared the initial bipolar statements of its members. A specific set of statements was then negotiated within each group. The sets of bipolar statements developed above were used as a basis for the second day of the program.

Each class member was asked to consider the description of effective teaching and learning for their focus class developed during the first part of the program. These descriptive statements, and their implied assumptions in relating to teaching and learning, were then considered by the class members. This set of statements formed the elements for the field of inquiry, or problem, being considered, namely describing effective teaching and learning.

These sets of statements were shared with other members of the group, using the same group membership as before. Individual members were given the opportunity to review and revise their statements. At this stage no attempt was made to negotiate a common set of statements, either within groups or with the whole class. This was done to try to ensure that the statements were clear for the individuals concerned, as this was considered vital to the next stage of presentation of the program. The statements so obtained were to be used as the elements of a repertory grid, the field of inquiry, or problem for which was the description of effective teaching and learning.

Introduction to Repertory Grid Techniques

Kelly's (1955) personal construct theory, its eleven corollaries and their implications for teaching and learning were discussed with the class. This discussion was based on the more detailed consideration given in Chapter 2 of this book.

The development and analysis of a repertory grid were discussed with the class. In particular, attention was paid to:

i   the notions of elements and constructs, and their distinction;
ii   the rehearsal of a preliminary exercise in developing and analyzing a repertory grid;
iii the procedures to be used for eliciting constructs;
iv   the procedures which can be used to develop a topic, or field of inquiry, with a group of teachers;
v   the notions of the initial and emergent poles of a construct;
vi   correlation procedures for both elements and constructs;
vii focusing the grid;
viii interpreting the grid.

The following is an example of the development and analysis of a repertory grid on descriptions of effective teaching and learning completed by one of the teachers in the course.

Example 1: Repertory Grid: Descriptive Statements (elements)

Elements: Statements of conditions for effective teaching and learning

A   Children learn most effectively when their individual needs are recognized.
B   Effective learning involves self-motivation.
C   Effective learning involves interaction between the teacher and the learner.
D   Children need to feel a sense of individual worth.
E   Effective learning involves practical experiences.
F   The learner should have a sense of purpose and direction.
G   The learning program should consider the whole child.
H   Children learn at different rates.
I   Active participation by the learner is necessary for effective learning.
J   Learners should evaluate their own learning needs.

Example 1: Initial Bipolar Statements (constructs)

Construct	Initial Pole	Emergent Pole
1	Effective learning involves interaction between the teacher and the learner	Effective learning involves the learner's own initatives
2	Effective learning depends on the individual learner's attitudes	Effective learning depends on the attitudes that develop from the relationship between teacher and learner
3	Effective learning is learner-centred	Effective learning requires teacher and learner input
4	Effective learning focuses on individual needs	Effective learning focuses on the needs of the curriculum
5	Effective learning is based on practical experiences	Effective learning precedes practical experiences
6	Effective learning needs to be purposeful for the learner	Effective learning needs to be purposeful for the teacher
7	Children learn at different rates	Children learn at the same rate
8	Effective learning involves self-evaluation by the learner	Effective learning involves external evaluation of the learner
9	Effective learning focuses on the whole child	Effective learning focuses on specific developmental areas of the child
10	The learner should be actively involved in the learning process	The learner should learn from a teacher model
11	Effective learning involves learner evaluation of learning performances and application to new situations	Effective learning involves learning behaviours established by the teacher

The repertory grid and the correlation matrices are shown in Tables 4.1, 4.2, 4.3 and 4.4.

Interpretation of the Repertory Grid

The teacher gave the following interpretation of this grid:

Example 1: Interpretation of a Repertory Grid
INITIAL ELEMENTS

Low Correlations
Elements A and B:
[The low correlation (6) was interpreted by the teacher to mean:]
'The teacher's perceived needs of the individual may not be seen by the individuals as being in their own best interests.'
[The remaining low correlations were interpreted by the teacher to mean:]

Elements B and C
The teacher–learner interaction does not always help to motivate the child. Does this mean that children would prefer a more structured, teacher–directed situation? This applies to my focus class, where their self–esteem is very low, and in order to motivate the group strong teacher input is necessary.

Elements A and F
This confirms the above, since recognition of needs did not correlate highly with the learner's sense of purpose. It also indicates a need to focus on self–esteem itself as an area of learning.

Elements B and G
If we are focusing on the whole child, we are focusing on his strengths and weaknesses. If we are asking children to focus on weaknesses, then it is a delicate issue for them to accept the weakness and become motivated to resolving it.

Elements C, I and J
The interaction places as much emphasis on the role of the teacher as it does on the role of the learner. I have a philosophy of the teacher as a facilitator of learning. With my focus class I provide more direction than I may in a different class. This is true of my

Table 4.1. Example 1: Repertory Grid for Descriptions of Effective Teaching and Learning —
Initial Bipolar Statements (constructs)

Construct	Initial pole	Emergent pole
1	Effective learning involves interaction between the teacher and the learner	Effective learning involves the learner's own initiatives
2	Effective learning depends on the individual learner's attitudes	Effective learning depends on the attitudes that develop from the relationship between teacher and learner
3	Effective learning is learner-centred	Effective learning requires teacher input
4	Effective learning focuses on individual needs	Effective learning focuses on the needs of the curriculum
5	Effective learning is based on practical experiences	Effective learning precedes practical experiences
6	Effective learning needs to be purposeful for the learner	Effective learning needs to be purposeful for the teacher
7	Children learn at different rates	Children learn at the same rate
8	Effective learning involves self-evaluation by the learner	Effective learning involves external evaluation of the learner
9	Effective learning focuses on the whole child	Effective learning focuses on specific developmental areas of the child
10	The learner should be actively involved in the learning process	The learner should learn from a teacher model
11	Effective learning involves learner evaluation of learning performances and application to new situations	Effective learning involves learning behaviours established by the teacher

teaching style. This is supported by low correlation between G and I, J.

High Correlations:
My argument to date is countered by these correlations. Perhaps this highlights a conflict between my teaching philosophy and my teaching style. It also indicates the fundamental importance of teacher–pupil relationships, and the difficulties the teacher has

Table 4.2. *Example 1: Repertory Grid for Descriptions of Effective Teaching and Learning*

Construct	A	B	C	D	E	F	G	H	I	J	Construct
1 Effective learning involves interaction between the teacher and the learner	✓	X	✓	✓	✓	X	✓	✓	X	X	Effective learning involves the learner's own initiatives
2 Effective learning depends on the individual learner's attitudes	X	✓	X	X	✓	✓	X	X	✓	✓	Effective learning depends on the attitudes that develop from the relationship between teacher and learner
3 Effective learning is learner-centred	X	✓	X	X	✓	✓	X	✓	✓	✓	Effective learning requires teacher input
4 Effective learning focuses on individual needs	✓	✓	✓	✓	✓	✓	✓	✓	✓	✓	Effective learning focuses on the needs of the curriculun
5 Effective learning is based on practical experiences	✓	✓	✓	✓	✓	✓	✓	✓	✓	✓	Effective learning precedes practical experiences
6 Effective learning needs to be purposeful for the learner	✓	✓	✓	✓	✓	✓	✓	✓	✓	✓	Effective learning needs to be purposeful for the teacher
7 Children learn at different rates	✓	✓	✓	✓	✓	✓	✓	✓	✓	✓	Children learn at the same rate
8 Effective learning involves self-evaluation by the learner	X	X	✓	X	X	✓	✓	✓	✓	✓	Effective learning involves external evaluation of the learner
9 Effective learning focuses on the whole child	✓	✓	✓	✓	✓	✓	✓	✓	✓	✓	Effective learning focuses on specific developmental areas of the child
10 The learner should be actively involved in the learning process	✓	✓	✓	✓	✓	✓	✓	✓	✓	✓	The learner should learn from a teacher model

Elements (Statements)

Table 4.3. Correlation Matrix for Elements

Elements	A	B	C	D	E	F	G	H	I	J
A		6	10	9	7	6	7	8	6	6
B			6	7	9	10	6	7	10	10
C				9	7	6	10	9	6	6
D					8	7	9	8	7	7
E						9	7	8	9	9
F							6	7	10	10
G								9	6	6
H									7	7
I										10
J										

Table 4.4. Correlation Matrix for Constructs

Constructs	1	2	3	4	5	6	7	8	9	10
1		1	2	6	6	6	6	2	6	6
2			9	5	5	5	5	9	5	5
3				6	6	6	6	8	6	6
4					10	10	10	6	10	10
5						10	10	6	10	10
6							10	6	10	10
7								6	10	10
8									6	6
9										10
10										

in meeting the needs of the individual as perceived by the individual, and as perceived by the teacher.

Low Correlations: Bipolar Statements (constructs)
Constructs 1 and 2
The low correlation can be explained by the way the poles were recorded. If construct 2's poles were reversed, then there would have been high correlation. Constructs 1 and 2 are similar and could have been combined.

Constructs 1 and 3
The low correlation reinforces the statements re teacher-learner input.

Constructs 1 and 8
The low correlation does not fit with my focus class where personal and immediate feedback is important. However, if we look at the two poles that do correlate, we see that there is a high correlation between learner-initiative and self-evaluation.

Constructs 2 and 5
Correlation occurs on the basis that learners' attitudes are related to learning based on practical experience, not on theory.

Constructs 2 and 6
Learner attitudes relate to recognition of learner needs, not curriculum needs.

Constructs 2 and 7
Learner attitudes relate to learning at different rates.

Constructs 4 and 8
Learning involves the learner being able to evaluate his own needs.

Constructs 5 and 8
Learners can best evaluate themselves through practical experiences.

Constructs 7 and 8
Learners need to judge the pace at which they can learn. They need to recognize their readiness for new learning situations.

Constructs 3 and 5
Learner-centred approach is best achieved by focusing on practical experiences.

Constructs 3 and 6
To be purposeful, learning needs to be learner-centred.

Constructs 3 and 9
Learner-centred means focusing on the whole child.

High Correlations
Constructs 4, 5, 6, 7, 9, 10 are integral parts of the educational philosophy as outlined in the Primary Education Report. For primary teachers these are fundamental to the learning process. As a result this only confirms my view of teaching. More value may have been gained by making the constructs less bipolar. This is necessary to enable a more critical look at the widely accepted beliefs outlines above.

Repertory Grid of Descriptions of Effective Teaching and Leaning

For each teacher, the set of statements describing effective teaching and learning was then used as the elements of a repertory grid. In this case the field of inquiry is the description of effective teaching and learning, and this field is represented by the set of descriptive statements, or elements, which relate to the class member's focus class. Bipolar statements (constructs) were then elicited from these elements, using the triad method as described in Chapter 2. Each of the poles of these statements was stated as a single, grammatically simple sentence.

The following is an example of the elicitation of bipolar statements, using the triad method. The three selected elements were:

A children learn most effectively when their individual needs are recognized;
B effective learning involves self-motivation;
C effective learning involves interaction between the teacher and the learner.

The first question to be asked, when using the triad method to elicit constructs, is: *Which two of the triad are similar in their implications for effective teaching and learning?* Having selected a pair of similar elements, say A and B, it must then be asked in what way they are similar. In this case both elements link learning to the individual. This similarity may then be stated as: *Effective learning is individually-based.* This is the initial pole of the bipolar statement or construct. The second question to be asked is: *In what way(s) are the pair A and B different from C?* In this case A and B stress the primary role of the individual in learning, whilst C stresses the importance of interaction. As the difference is this emphasis on interaction, the emergent pole may be stated as: *Effective learning is based on the interaction between the teacher and learner.* The bipolar statements (or construct) elicited are, therefore: *Effective learning is individually based. Effective learning is based on the interaction between teacher and learner.*

In this way each teacher elicited an initial set of bipolar statements, or constructs. These were shared with groups, using the same group membership as before. The aim of this sharing was to enable each teacher to add to, delete, or modify their initial set of bipolar statements. The revised sets of bipolar statements were shared with the whole class to allow individual teachers to review and revise their particular set of bipolar statements. Each group was then asked to share and negotiate an agreed set of bipolar statements relating to descriptions of effective teaching and learning. Following this, each teacher displayed the elements and bipolar statements in the form of a repertory grid.

Using the procedures discussed in Chapter 2, each teacher completed a correlation analysis for both elements and bipolar statements. On the basis of these analyses each teacher attempted to focus their repertory grid by rewriting both the elements and bipolar statements of higher correlation adjacent to one another in the grid. In most cases it was not necessary to do this manually. The focusing could be done through the inspection of closely related elements and bipolar statements.

The element and bipolar statement correlations were then considered by each teacher for their particular repertory grid. These correlations were then interpreted by the teacher as they related to their focus class. Each teacher then stated their interpretation of their grid. These interpretations were then shared within the class groups, and there was an opportunity to review and revise the interpretations of the individual grids. At this stage no further sharing or negotiation of interpretation was attempted.

To build on the approach to describing effective teaching and learning already developed, the following approach to reading relevant articles and texts was developed and discussed with the class.

A Suggested Guide to Reading
The emphasis of this course is on the descriptions of effective

teaching and learning used by teachers. The readings given for the course should, as well as proposing and arguing a range of viewpoints concerning curriculum planning and development, provide a range of alternative descriptions through which effective teaching and learning can be described. Two approaches to reading are suggested. The first is based on procedures for developing repertory grids, whilst the second uses sets of key questions relating to educating, teaching and learning.

The Repertory Grid Approach

The use of repertory grids to analyze and interpret a particular reading depends upon both elements and constructs (in this case bipolar statements) being elicited from the field of inquiry, that is from the article.

Analysis and interpretation of possible relationships between the elements and bipolar statements, elicited from these elements, may be undertaken using repertory grid techniques.

For each reading it will be necessary to elicit, initially, a set of elements, which are representative of the full range of arguments advanced in that reading. That is, a set of statements (elements) giving a coherent and complete summary of the central arguments of the reading must be made.

To develop this summary, it may help to begin by considering the structure of the reading. If, for example, it is presented in clearly differentiated sections, it may be advisable to summarize, separately, each section. These summaries may be consolidated to give a full summary of the article. If it is not sectionalized, it may be helpful to consider, separately, each paragraph. In this case, the integration of the essential arguments of each paragraph will lead to a final summary. These procedures should enable a coherent and succinct summary of the article to be written.

This summary may be used for eliciting the elements for a repertory grid. For this purpose, the summary must be written as a connected series of grammatically simple sentences. For the purposes of later analysis, it is preferable that not more than 10 sentences be used. When formed, these sentences should be modified, if necessary, to avoid overlap and inconsistency. The final set of sentences will be the elements representing the article being studied.

The elements should be listed, and a triad method used to elicit constructs as bipolar statements. Such bipolar statements will reflect the alternative descriptions being used by the author in relation to the particular issues being addressed in the reading. A sufficient set of bipolar statements should be elicited to represent adequately the educational issues being raised in the reading.

The set of elements and bipolar constructs forms a repertory grid. Correlation analyses of both elements and bipolar statements may now be completed. These will indicate possible relationships within both the set of elements, and the set of bipolar statements. In this way, a focused grid may be produced.

The focused grid may be used as a basis for interpreting the reading being studied. It will assist in considering the alternative descriptions of issues being used, and the assumptions that appear to underlie these alternative descriptions, and the possible consequences of describing the issues in these ways. In examining a particular reading in this way, the emphasis is on the descriptions of effective teaching and learning implied by the reading, and the consequences of alternative descriptions for curriculum planning and development.

The Key Questions Approach

A second approach is to consider the reading using a set of key questions. In this case, each class member proposes a set of general questions relating to effective teaching and learning. These may be shared with other class members and an agreed set of key questions negotiated. Such a set may include, for example, questions relating to:

    i   the conditions for effective learning;
   ii   the motivating of students;
  iii   the conditions for effective teaching;
   iv   the purposes of educating;
   v   the types, and nature, of knowledge that the students should acquire;
   vi   the organization of the curriculum;
  vii   the teaching resources available;
 viii   the social expectations for the students;
   ix   the key principles and concepts used in discussing teaching and learning.

By considering these questions in relation to a particular article, additional questions will be generated. The range of possible answers obtained by applying these questions to a particular reading may be used to examine alternative descriptions of effective teaching and learning.

Summary

Whichever approach is used, the emphasis should be on gaining further insights into the descriptions used for effective teaching and learning.

Each of the above approaches was discussed with the class. The approaches were then demonstrated using the reading 'Curriculum Development and Student-centredness' (see Chapter 3). The class was then asked to apply these approaches to the following readings: L.A. Reid (1981) 'Knowledge, Knowing and Becoming Educated', *Journal of Curriculum Studies*, 13, 2, pp. 78–82; P.H. Hirst (1974) 'Liberal Education and the Nature of Knowledge', *Knowledge and the Curriculum* (London: Routledge and Kegan Paul), pp. 30–33.

During the second stage of the program the teachers focused on approaches to curriculum development by considering the notion of liberal education. The examination of the notion of liberal education led to the identification of some philosophical issues as being critical to the discussion of the educational justification of liberal education. The implications of each of these issues for effective teaching and learning, and particularly for alternative descriptions of affective teaching and learning, were considered.

Course Content

To do so, readings presented under the following headings were considered:

    i   curricula and liberal education;
   ii   Hirst's Forms of Knowledge;
  iii   intellectual development and the Forms of Knowledge;
   iv   objectivity, truth and intersubjective agreement;
    v   procedural and propositional knowledge;
   vi   Polanyi, objectivism and tacit integration.

For each of these, a prepared reading was made available. Each reading concluded with a statement of the key questions raised in the reading, and a set of bipolar statements, which attempted to summarize some of the important philosophical issues raised by these questions.

For each reading:

    i   each class member was asked to identify the key educational issues or questions it raised, particularly as these related to effective teaching and learning;

    ii   share these questions or issues within groups and negotiate an agreed list of questions or issues for the group;

    iii the sets of group questions were shared with the whole class, and a consolidated list of questions or issues negotiated;

    iv each teacher was asked to consider the bipolar statements implied by each of the questions or issues, using the triad method, either in the group set of negotiated issues or questions or the class set of issues or questions;

    v   in either case, the sets of bipolar statements were shared with the group, and a negotiated set of statements developed;

    vi the implications of each pair of bipolar statements for describing effective teaching and learning were considered by the group;

    vii the bipolar statements were rewritten within the groups as alternative descriptions of effective teaching and learning;

    viii each teacher was asked to review and revise the bipolar statements with a view to describing effective teaching and learning for their focus class;

    ix this set of bipolar statements, and the final set of issues or questions for the reading, was recorded by each student.

After all readings have been completed:

    x   each group was asked to produce a consolidated list of questions or issues, and bipolar statements, for the total set of reading considered.

At the end of this stage of the course

    xi the teachers restated their descriptions of effective teaching and learning as these applied to their focus class;

    xii this restatement was used to produce a set of elements describing effective teaching and learning;

    xiii the triad method was used to elicit bipolar statements from these elements;

    xiv correlation matrices for both elements and bipolar statements were completed;

    xv if necessary, the repertory grid was focused;

xvi analysis and interpretation of this grid in terms of describing effective teaching and learning was completed;

xvii this interpretation was compared with that obtained at the end of the first week of the course.

It should be noted that, in conducting the program in the manner outlined above, the teaching approach used during the first stage of the course has been retained. That is, the conduct of the program was based upon the following activities:

i describing issues and questions;
ii recognizing these as key issues and questions to be addressed;
iii exploring alternative descriptions of these issues and questions;
iv sharing these alternative descriptions;
v negotiating an agreed set of descriptions;
vi reviewing and testing these descriptions, and, if necessary, revising them, in this case in relation to the focus class.

The class was then introduced to the program readings. These readings were discussed in detail with the class, and alternative descriptions of effective teaching and learning were explored. These alternative descriptions were stated as bipolar statements.

During the third phase of the program readings given in Module C, relating to a range of approaches to curriculum development, were considered. The approaches considered were:

i curriculum development and objectives;
ii curriculum development and student abilities;
iii curriculum development and student-centredness;
iv curriculum development and educational processes;
v curriculum development and conservation.

For each of these readings:

i each teacher was asked to consider the reading and to state the key issues or questions raised by it (these issues or questions are the elements which represent the reading);
ii these questions were shared within the groups, and an agreed set of elements, describing effective teaching and learning, was negotiated within the group;
iii each student used these elements to elicit a set of bipolar statements;

iv these bipolar statements were shared within the group, and an agreed set of such statements was negotiated;

v   each student completed a repertory grid using these elements and bipolar statements;

vi correlation matrices for both elements and constructs were completed, and where necessary the repertory grid was focused;

vii the repertory grid was then analyzed and interpreted in relation to effective teaching and learning for the focus class.

After the completion of each reading a short review session was held with the whole class.

The approach to conducting the program as outlined above was retained throughout the procedure for each reading. That is, the activities of describing, recognizing, exploring, sharing, negotiating and reviewing and revising were all contained within the way the course was conducted for this week.

Student Evaluation of the Program

After the analysis and interpretation each student wrote a detailed evaluative statement of the entire program. In doing so, they reflected upon the purposes of the program and the extent to which these were, or were not, met by their participation in the course. In particular, each student commented on:

i   the strengths of the course in relation to achieving the stated objectives;

ii   the weaknesses of the course;

iii those aspects of the course which they considered to be of particular professional assistance, and the reasons for them being so;

iv   those elements of the course which did not give professional assistance;

v   the approach to conducting the course as a possible model for teacher development;

vi   the notion of professional development assumed by the course and its conduct;

vii the use of repertory grids as a means of helping teachers describe effective teaching and learning;

viii the idea of a focus class as a basis for a course in teacher development;

ix the course readings supplied as a basis for the discussion of educational issues, and hence for teacher development;

x the approach to assessing taken for the course;

xi the ways in which the course should be modified or changed for future classes;

xii the likely long-term effects of the program.

The materials produced during the program by three of the participants, in particular, the repertory grids and their analyses and interpretations which relate directly to describing effective teaching and learning, will be considered in the next chapter.

Chapter 5

Meeting Individual and
Group Purposes

This chapter reports a detailed evaluation of the use of the touchstone approach for the teacher development program, and discusses the implications of this approach. The evaluation is based on the teachers' responses to a series of questions relating to their experience of, and reflections on, the teacher development program. Responses to each of these questions are discussed and reported, and suggestions are made as to how the touchstone approach may be consolidated and improved.

The purposes of the teacher development program for the individual teachers participating in it were to develop each participant's capacities to:

i   recognize and describe;
ii   explore;
iii   review; and
iv   revise and clarify

alternative frames of reference which they might use to describe effective teaching and learning; that is, to state their personal theories of teaching and learning. The teachers worked in groups, the purposes of this group work being to develop each participant's capacities to:

i   communicate;
ii   share; and
iii   negotiate

these frames of reference, and hence personal theories of teaching and learning, with the other participants.

To assist in the evaluation of the extent to which the teacher development program met the individual and group purposes of the participants, the teachers were asked to respond to the following evaluation questions.

    i   What were the strengths of the touchstone approach?

    ii   What were the difficulties of this approach?

    iii   What was the professional worth of the program?

    iv   What were the advantages of developing a dialogical approach to teacher development?

    v   What were the advantages and disadvantages of the use of repertory grids in promoting a critical dialogue on teaching and learning, and in monitoring and assessing changes in the intelligibility of teachers' personal theories of teaching and learning?

    vi   What were the strengths and weaknesses of the input provided by the readings on approaches to curriculum development in promoting a critically reflective discourse on teaching and learning?

    vii   What were the advantages and disadvantages of using a focus class as a practical reference point for monitoring and assessing the practical plausibility of the dialogue, and, in particular, of teacher's personal theories of teaching and learning for the focus class?

    viii   What were the advantages of the professional journal as a mode of assessment for teachers participating in the program?

    ix   What modifications will be necessary to ensure the effectiveness of the touchstone approach in meeting the individual and group purposes of the program?

    x   What, for the participants, are the likely long-term effects of the program?

First, in commenting on the strengths of the touchstone approach many of the participating teachers stated that they had been challenged to recognize and review their current practices, particularly through the presentation of alternative means of educating, teaching and learning, Whilst this challenge was appreciated in stimulating them to clarify their thinking, their personal theories of teaching, several teachers maintained that, despite this challenge, they had not changed their fundamental beliefs about teaching and learning. In seeking this clarification the teachers agreed that they had been confronted with 'a host of ideas, insights and attitudes of "substance", rather than platitudes'. Typically, one teacher saw as two significant aspects of the program:

Introspection demanded of the participants, in both the areas of theory and practices. This approach served well the purposes of promoting motivation and maintaining interest through the constancy of the course's 'visible' relevance.

and

The group dynamics, both at the 'macro' and 'micro' levels, generated a number of valuable spin-offs. The input of educators from a variety of backgrounds, styles and responsibilities, frequently enhanced the quality of debate and review. Most interestingly, despite this range and diversity, it seemed that the issues were more clarified, and even conflicts resolved.

For this teacher, the course was successful at two levels. Teachers had been led to a mutually understood dialogue, which enabled them to communicate in a meaningful way, and this should provide for an optimism that an exercise such as this program should have have some chance of success in the usually more restricted educational climate of one's own school.

Furthermore, many of the participants saw the program as clarifying the link between teaching and the curriculum, and between teacher development and curriculum development. As another commented, the program strengthened his capacity to link educational theory and practice.

My initial attempts at describing effective teaching and learning were, on reflection, rather clumsy, and without a basis of sound understanding of the theory as it translates into practice. As I reflected on these statements . . . , I realized how much the course had clarified for me the link between curriculum development and teacher development. My background in the theory of curriculum development was too general, and the links had not been made in a clear way between theory and practice. Secondly, the course helped me to recognize the way in which I was looking at 'the school' — more in terms of organizational development and professional development rather than improvements in teaching and learning, which might come through curriculum development and professional development. I believe the link between these three aspects was not strong enough previously, possibly also this was attributable to a heavy emphasis in previous courses on professional and organizational development.

This linkage was seen as crucial for total school development, and an understanding of it as essential to the confidence and enthusiasm necessary for senior teachers in providing school leadership in teaching and learning. In support of this another stated:

> I feel the purposes of the course ... have been well supported. I found the model for the course — the relationship between curriculum development, teacher development and organizational development — particularly interesting, and the starting point for the course excellent. I feel I have had the opportunity to look at alternative curriculum models, and to recognize some of my own beliefs in them. Certainly, I have a much clearer understanding of my own underlying assumptions about teaching and learning.

An understanding of teaching and learning is, of course, dependent upon the capacity to describe it intelligibly, and to communicate these descriptions to others. Participating teachers were strong in the belief that the program had helped them become clearer and more succinct in their descriptions. Whilst this had occurred, the changes were slow and needed the full three weeks of the program. During the three weeks teachers became increasingly aware that such changes were taking place, often subtly, tentatively and gradually. Many saw the grid, and the challenge of interpreting it, as a major factor in helping this change.

In addition, participants agreed that a major factor in bringing about such changes is the opportunity to discuss, share, reflect and negotiate with other teachers. This aspect was enthusiastically supported by all. A typical comment was: 'Another advantage has been the cohesiveness and support within the group, and the ease of forming subgroups for various purposes. The wide range of levels represented by the participants was of real value in ordering perspectives towards the learning process.'

Similarly, the continuing need to focus back to the practice of teaching was strongly supported. Typical of the supportive comments made by the teachers is the following:

> The main strength of the course, in supporting its objective of presenting 'teachers with a range of alternative ways in which they can construe their experience of teaching and learning', was that it did provide this experience for me. Through the process of looking at ideas and theories, which initially seemed far removed

from the classroom and my own experiences, and working through the process of relating these *back* to my experience, I gradually established a greater depth of professional reflection, professional dialogue, and established educationally meaningful ways of looking at, and discussing, my actual classroom experiences.

This is borne out when I compare my initial statements, or elements of effective teaching and learning, written at the beginning of the course, and my interpretation of these, to the same elements rewritten at the end of the course, which show my ideas have become more succinct, better expressed, educationally, and give me a greater insight into the gaps between my educational ideas and actual classroom practices. It has also provided me with a clearer set of educational ideals which I now feel I have begun to put into practice. In other words, as the course objective stated, I was able to establish my frames of reference much more clearly, and did appreciate the opportunities of being able to negotiate them with others, and review and revise them.

Kelly's view of 'man as a personal scientist' with an orientation to act in terms of predictions of the future is very much in sympathy with modern management practices which stress the key role of visions of the future in guiding decision-making. The teacher development program should, therefore, help teachers to develop a future orientation towards their practice. This change of orientation from being merely reactive to present problems to planning on the basis of perceived futures occurred for many of the teachers. Illustrative of this is the comment:

There is no doubt in my mind the course has caused me to look not only at my role as a teacher but also as a curriculum coordinator. The process of using the repertory grids as a review medium has achieved the objective of highlighting *the need to review with respect to future orientation*. The course has generated within me a desire to look forward and put into practice some ideas generated during the duration of the course.

In the program the individual and group purposes were to develop the participant's capacities to:

    i   recognize and describe;
   ii   explore;
  iii   review;

    iv   revise and clarify;
    v   communicate;
    vi   share; and
    vii negotiate.

the frames of reference used to describe effective teaching and learning for their focus class.

An examination of each of the responses of the teachers revealed that all believed that the program purposes had been achieved. As well as meeting these purposes, teachers saw other advantages in the program. These included:

    i   an increased capacity to describe effective teaching and learning succinctly;
    ii   an enhanced ability to communicate with colleagues, particularly in describing effective teaching and learning;
    iii the consistent relevance of the program;
    iv   the enhancement of the quality of debate and review by a variety of educational inputs from other participants;
    v   facilitating and clarifying links between theory and practice;
    vi   helping the recognition of the link between teacher, organization and curriculum development;
    vii new insights into the ways in which teachers might change and improve their professional skills;
    viii providing a clear set of educational ideals on personal educational philosophy;
    ix   a clearer understanding of personal assumptions regarding teaching and learning.

Of the difficulties mentioned by the teachers the major problem occurred with the development and interpretation of the repertory grids. The main difficulty was in preparing elements and eliciting constructs that gave a meaningful focus on the issues being discussed. However, participants saw a variety of reasons for this, and made appropriate positive suggestions to overcome these difficulties. Teachers' comments included:

The course presented me with some problems of understanding with regard to the interpretation of the grids. (This may not be a fault of the course, as anything that is new worries me when I cannot understand it first up.) Perhaps a mock up of elements and constructs and a grid for a class could have been presented and discussed with the whole group or small groups at the beginning of the course. This may have allowed me to immediately see the purpose of the repertory grid.

Sufficient time to become accustomed to their use was an important factor. Another teacher commented:

Although I gained a great deal from using the Repertory Grid process in looking at my views of teaching and learning, I would eventually like to be able to use another process. Given the time that we had, and the material and issues we covered, I recognize that the period of time was just enough to become confident in using such as process.

A further difficulty was the interpretation of the grids. Both of these problems were largely overcome by the end of the third week. This was achieved by the lecturer drawing the groups together to reinforce the best method of approach, and also to remind members that they ought to group issues wherever possible to get a broader view of what the analysis indicated. The lecturer's constant individual counselling during this period was invaluable.

My only suggestion of an improvement of this approach would possibly be the production of a model which would encompass elements, constructs, matrices, and, in particular, an analysis of the results. I feel that this would be of value. However, I recognize that the danger of this is to lock people into a set way of analyzing an issue, which conforms to the model.

Whilst the importance of the thinking processes stimulated by the use of repertory grids was not denied, there were several suggestions that similar but alternative processes might be used. These suggestions included: 'The reliance on the repertory grid denies the importance of exploring in various ways. In the same way that it is important to explore alternative frames of reference, it is important to do so through a variety of methods.' And 'although the repertory grid approach was a successful professional development exercise, it may have "lightened" the course a little to have other methods or "processes" as well.' In summary, the difficulties identified were:

    i   difficulties experienced in developing and interpreting the repertory grids;

  ii difficulties with some of the language used in the readings for
      the program;
  iii the gap between the theory presented in the readings and actual
      classroom practice.

The difficulties with the use and interpretation of repertory grids
may be overcome be a more detailed and comprehensive introduction.
The style of thinking required, and particularly the elicitation of constructs and their bipolar nature, was different from that previously
experienced by most of the teachers. This difficulty is one of teaching,
rather than being inherent in the theory and application of repertory
grids.

If the teacher is to be challenged with new ideas and alternative
perspectives on teaching and learning, this will necessarily involve the use
of new language. Challenging current ideas and perspectives must be
mediated, in part, through the language used. This perceived difficulty
does, however, draw attention to the crucial need to pay attention to the
language used in teacher development programs. In essence, it draws
attention to the thrust of this book, namely, that it is the enhancement of
the intelligibility of our discourse on teaching which is at the heart of
teacher development.

Perhaps the dilemmas faced by the teachers in this program are
highlighted by the following comment of one of the participants.

> The major weakness of the course is that it does not directly
> impinge on the teaching situation. In clearing my thinking re-
> garding the teaching-learning situation, and developing a set of
> ideals, it has tended to do so in isolation from the actual class-
> room. The focus class helped to bring things back to this level,
> but in reality for me, as the course progressed it became more and
> more difficult to take my thinking back to the real-life teaching
> situation, and for me this was a contradiction to what I wanted
> from the course. Module B was especially instrumental in taking
> me away from this reality. However, Module C helped overcome
> this problem and brought things more into perspective, and, on
> reflection, back to reality for me. In retrospect, this weakness that
> I have identified was only a weakness because I brought precon-
> ceived expectations. In looking at the outcomes, now, I can see a
> great value in this method of reaching a set of ideals, because I
> now have a good basis for reflective thinking when justifying my
> approaches to teaching and learning.

As far as the overall professional worth of the program was concerned, the teachers were able to offer a balanced view. Several of these comments speak very clearly. As one said:

> I have been assisted professionally because I was continually challenged to assess my position on teaching and learning. (Was I actually doing what I believed I was doing?) During the course I was able to discuss these thoughts with staff (of my school), and to challenge them to question their own approaches to teaching and learning. I do not believe I would have questioned this matter as deeply had I not been introduced to repertory grids, and their implications for teaching and learning.
>
> When working in groups, I found the discussions with colleagues from the secondary area challenging and helpful, particularly when interpreting the grids. (Peer teaching certainly worked for me!) I also found that I had something to share with them regarding organization and approaches to child-centred learning. The mode of working in smaller groups allows for the freer expression of ideas and risk taking, exactly the model for a holistic approach to teaching and learning.
>
> Throughout the course, I often challenged the worth of using the repertory grid, but I could see that there was value in the exercise. We did express thoughts in the groups that we may not use the grids as such in schools, but I believe they have been of benefit and we would not have to complete them as fully when reviewing particular aspects of teaching and learning.

For another teacher:

> My professional development from this course is twofold. Firstly, as a teacher it has made me reflect on my own educational philosophy. It was obvious from some of the interpretations of the work I covered I am in conflict, and that I question and need to evaluate more closely what I believe in teaching.
>
> This personal review would, hopefully, enable me to go through a process with other staff to evaluate one's own school philosophy, the classroom practices, that are evident in the school that I am in.
>
> As part of my position there is a need for me to converse with parents, members of the teaching profession and other

people involved in the community at large about educational theory. Because of my reflection during this course I am sure I will be able to reflect a more accurate degree of educational philosophy.

A third teacher commented:

In essence, the course alerted me to a number of basic requirements for curriculum development, and provided insights into some useful methods suitable for such activity.

The quintessential requisite of establishing some common level of agreement by staff before curriculum negotiation can begin was appropriately highlighted, and its priority is clearly understood. The necessity for obtaining such accord would not have been appreciated in the past. Better than this was the exposure to a device for finding the necessary areas of agreement.

Concomitant with this was the insight gained on the importance of language and terminology when the curriculum is under discussion. The basic necessity of ensuring such language is 'common' in meaning to, and understanding by, all was enlightening, particularly if the educational dialogue is to be meaningful and productive.

At a psychological level an outcome from the course would be a greater personal confidence and certainty; this together with a much clearer perspective of the future for teaching should produce a more effective learning situation.

A fourth teacher wrote:

In the first instance, the nature of the group provided an excellent basis for professional growth. The cross-section of people from a variety of educational institutions, and at various stages of experience and positions of responsibility, have contributed to a broad view of education being elucidated rather than a focus on particular issues.

I found the selection of readings provided gave a basis for discussion which, while theoretical, was easily applicable to the school and classroom. The contrasting views given stimulated the group and enabled, or forced, members to identify their beliefs with positions held by the range of writings. Also, the paper prepared by the lecturer, and used as the medium for elucidating the repertory grid was concise and stimulating. The method of writing employed made the task of developing elements and constructs much simpler.

The strong professional impact of the program is evident from comments such as the following:

> Yes, a very good approach and requiring a great deal of soul searching. Most people could not help be aware of the depth at which they looked at their reasons for teaching in their particular style, and I feel no one could remain unaltered after the course. The repertory grid technique is very useful for this 'self-examination', and soul searching, and it has the serendipity effect of finding out the 'tutor' no matter how you try and cover it up. This comes about by the cross-referencing of constructs and elements and forcing the participant to look at 'alternative' methods. If you believe this then it presupposes an alternative method, and you can take your position in the continuum. Therefore, the strength of the approach is in 'stripping down' the various layers of your beliefs, and making you aware of why you hold these, rather than taking a body of knowledge and adding that to your personally held body of knowledge as other courses have done. It was a critical analysis that was also effective.

> Professional people with valuable ideas and experiences, which would be built upon and related back to theories, rather than a set of theories being examined for its own sake as a valuable body of knowledge for all teachers to acquire. Obviously, if this was the assumption, then the idea of groups and individual contributions as opposed to a didactic approach, would actually follow from this.

> The use of small groups meant that all members had the opportunity to participate, whereas in larger groups the conversation tends to be dominated by one or two individuals, as I recently experienced in another course. Thus, as mentioned previously, the individual feels his contribution is recognized and valued.

> One of the most fascinating aspects for me was the subtle way in which our lecturer's point of view slowly emerged and was not really made clear to me until the end of the course. It was only then that I had become familiar with his particular bias. How-

ever, it became obvious that we had been *gently* led through this particular bias, during the course, so that a great many of us found ourselves looking towards a particular teaching style which was *more* student-centred and took less account of the subject approach to curriculum development.

In summary, the program participants were enthusiastic in their support for the approach taken. In particular, the following positive features were emphasized.

   i   The program used an adult learning theory.

   ii   The style, content and method of the program did not create any feelings of inadequacy among the participants.

   iii   The teaching of the program was developmental, and encouraged a focus on practice.

   iv   The approach appeared to be more valid than other models of professional development which some participants had used.

   v   Small group activity was particularly valuable.

   vi   The repertory grid technique was useful for 'self-examination and soul searching'.

   vii   The strength of the approach was in 'stripping down the various layers of your beliefs and making you aware of why you hold these, rather than taking a body of knowledge and adding that to your personally held body of knowledge.'

   viii   '. . . the underlying assumption behind the conducting of the course was that we were all professional people with valuable ideas and experiences, which could be built on and related *back* to theories, rather than a set of theories being examined for its own sake.'

   ix   The approach involved 'a particular teaching style which was *more* student-centred and took less account of the subject approach to curriculum development.'

   x   The course demands 'a degree of commitment by participants'.

   xi   The 'emphasis on learning linked with organization and staff development' was considered most appropriate.

   xii   The conduct of the program assumed that all participants would be 'active' and 'have a worthwhile contribution to make'.

   xiii   'The curriculum [of the program] was allowed to flow and ebb to meet the needs of the learner (participant).'

   xiv   'Assessment was individual learner [participant] based.'

xv   The direction of the program was maintained by subtle suggestions and provision of alternatives.

This approach to teacher development is dialogical. As such, it is
dependent on teachers working in groups to share, review and revise
their personal and group theories of teaching, and to express these as part
of an expanding and increasingly intelligible dialogue on teaching and
learning. The role of group sharing and revision is crucial to this process.
Many of the participants' comments illustrated their awareness and appreciation of the significance of group dialogue. The following were typical
comments: 'The collective analysis of study topics, the different points of
view, and particularly interpretation, did much to broaden not only the
issues under review, but each participant's outlook on it.' Another was:
'The atmosphere of cohesiveness quickly evident facilitated, in a significant way, the gaining of insights by members.... The phenomenon
of how group members, relatively quickly, assimilated the "finesse" of
dealing with the educational language was enlightening.' Moreover, '...
despite the nature of the group with its diversity of interests and backgrounds, which itself yielded insights and perspectives, the course and the
objective of meaningful discourse by a varied group of educators had not
only been encouragingly achieved, but was evidence of a suitable model
[for teacher development].'

The dialogical nature of this approach to teacher development
emphasizes group sharing, review and revision of insights on teaching
and learning. This, in turn, highlights the significance of both group
membership (who belongs to which groups and when and why) and how
this membership is changed to optimize teacher development for both the
individual teacher and for the whole group of teachers participating in the
program. As one teacher commented: '... from using such a model the
process would grow to the point that whole group negotiation would
occur. It is also important that, within a staff, people get the opportunity
to relate to all members through changing group structures or similar
on different issues.' Furthermore, 'The wisdom of the corporate body
seemed to inevitably result in elements and constructs tighter in thought,
more relevant in application and sufficiently broad to allow for acceptance
by all group members.'

A further requirement of the touchstone approach is that, given
the assumption of a holistic epistemology, theory development should
proceed through open and critical communication. The meeting of this
requirement was evident from the comments of the teachers, and is,
perhaps, best summarized by one teacher's statement that 'I think that it
has been an excellent model that has produced a tight, professional,

supporting group, who were totally honest with their feelings and attitudes about teaching and learning.' Furthermore, 'Because interaction (and hence dialogue) formed the basis of the program, the learner was continually being confronted and freed to react. To do so effectively has caused a clarity of thinking, and the development of skills in conversation in the area of effective teaching and learning.'

In summary, the dialogical nature of the touchstone approach to teacher development was seen by the participating teachers in the following ways. First, the success of the touchstone approach and, in particular, the development of a more intelligible dialogue on teaching and learning, depend, as one teacher put it, on a 'non-threatening and open-way'. In this way the processes of the program, and specifically group interaction, could grow to a point where whole group negotiation, such as for a school teaching staff, could occur. When this happened, the approach was seen by the teachers as having the potential to broaden and clarify discussion not only of the issue under review, but also of each teacher's outlook, or personal beliefs and theories, about the issue.

Through the dialogue promoted by the touchstone approach group cohesiveness will be achieved, but the intelligibility of this dialogue will be both widened and enhanced in clarity if regular changes in the membership of the various contributing groups are made. With these changes, group interaction will be stimulated and the input of alternative points of view on teaching and learning promoted. Such groups would, desirably, include a blend of teaching approaches, with a balance between, for instance, lectures, question sessions, general discussion with the whole group and some opportunity for teachers to work in pairs and individually.

For these teachers, the most valuable aspects of the dialogical nature of the touchstone approach to teacher development were:

i   the group discussion of issues;
ii   the associated high level and openness of the conversations of these groups;
iii   the input of a wide range of alternative perspectives on teaching and learning;
iv   enhanced opportunites to consider, in an open and critical way, the advantages and disadvantages of a diversity of educational theories;
v   the respect for the individual contributions of the participating teachers;
vi   the strong emphasis on the dialogical processes;
vii   the concern for overall teacher development as compared with

development focused on specific aspects of a teacher's work such as teacher planning.

A major feature of the touchstone approach, as applied to the teacher development program, is the use of repertory grids as a means of both promoting and clarifying dialogue on teaching and learning, and in monitoring and assessing any enhancement of the intelligibility of this dialogue. Whilst the use of repertory grids is a powerful means of achieving these purposes, their effective use by teachers is somewhat problematic. For the participating teachers, considerable effort, and some frustration, was experienced before their use for these purposes was easily and effectively attained. This is borne out by the teachers' comments when asked about the advantages and disadvantages of repertory grids. Amongst these comments were:

> Throughout the course I often challenged the use of the repertory grid, but I could see there was value in its use. We did express thought in the group that we may not use the grids, as such, in the schools, but I believe they have been of benefit, and we would not have to complete them as fully when reviewing particular aspects of teaching and learning.

Another teacher said:

> Using the grid over the three weeks of the course I have been able to reflect on my teaching practices and philosophies. This process is good in that, after time, I was able to do it efficiently and was able to reflect. However, I would find it difficult to use with staff because of the time it does require. Thus frustration would perhaps interfere with the purposes.

But for others, the dilemmas about the use of the grids remained, as typified by the following statement of an obviously perplexed teacher.

> While being prepared to accept the claims for their practical usefulness — at least for an experienced operator — when applied to a variety of situations this component of the course brought most discomfort for me. This may be because they involve demanding mental exercises, or at least so when used in such a 'jargon' filled world as teaching, or one wonders whether they suit better when background skills are held. It is appreciated that they provide a systematic way of examining a number of problems, and that

they are most successful in making us work at ourselves as teachers.

However, the feeling of unease remains at the close of the course, and this I regret. Perhaps the idea of a model may have helped by more quickly making their operations understood. Although I can see myself using them at a rather fundamental level of incidental construct placement, I feel inadequately prepared to apply them myself in the future — at least at the time of writing. This reticence, I regret.

Many of the comments made by the teachers as they attempted to come to terms with the use of repertory grids, and to understand their difficulties in relation to them, are very insightful. In particular, they reveal the intensely personal nature of teachers' beliefs about teaching and learning, how threatening challenges to these beliefs are, and how extremely difficult it is for teachers to change their personal theories of teaching and to translate these changes into teaching practices. These issues are encapsulated by the teacher who commented:

Because repertory grids were new to the group it took some time for most of us to come to terms with what was being attempted. This applied particularly to the development of constructs and the analysis of the grids. Once we had had some experience in trial-ling this approach it became apparent that repertory grids were valuable as a method of analyzing our thoughts and beliefs. The grids enabled us to go back to a fundamental position with regard to teaching and learning. It was this simplicity that I found useful as it gave a practical insight into the relationship between theory and classroom practice. The ordering of one's thinking is quite difficult without some sort of structure such as that provided by the grids. I think that it is important to note that the benefits are largely personal, and, if introduced as a staff exercise, could provide considerable threat to staff members. The exercise whereby we analyzed pieces of literature would, perhaps, be a good group exercise so that the techniques would not be open to public scrutiny.

Whilst the use of repertory grids as a basis for promoting a critically reflective dialogue on teaching and learning remained problematic to varying degrees for all of the participants, an awareness and appreciation of their power in developing this dialogue also emerged strongly. Typically, the teachers commented that whilst they were initially not keen on using the grids, as the program developed their effectiveness became more apparent. They began to be seen as a relatively non-threatening way of reflecting on their thinking and preferred practice, and, in particular, through the need for interpreting both the elements and constructs of the grid, as an additional focus for reviewing and revising personal theories of teaching. Likewise, the need to develop bipolar constructs meant that the teachers were asked to consider alternative educational theories, particularly contrasting perspectives of teaching and learning. Not only did the process of eliciting bipolar constructs assist the critical exploration of alternative personal theories of teaching and learning, but, as was emphasized by several of the teachers, it

> ... forces the development of a new discourse or conversation so that the teachers can converse, and, hopefully, reach agreement or a starting point.... Over a period of time I found that my frames of reference had changed, and that the technique does provide a 'non-threatening' vehicle for discourse, it provides a language generator, and it provides a means of stripping off the assumptions as people have to lay bare the true frames of reference.

In support of this comment another teacher said:

> It is not until the process has been completed that, as if by magic, the main points of one's thinking are succinctly revealed. This is the only method I have personally experienced, which enables me to so clearly relate theories back to my actual personal educational beliefs and practices. Even though I find the process not always attractive, the end point is very worthwhile as a means of reducing theory to practice.

Perhaps the most wholehearted and insightful support is shown by the following teacher response:

> The repertory grid made me distil one's thoughts. By providing a framework it made one more comfortable with the analysis process. It has given me a set of beliefs as to what I see as fundamental to me and to my teaching. It clarified that to get agreement between different views then you have to go back to a common ground and work for these.

It can be used in a very simple, and non-threatening way. It makes you order your thinking; it allows you to compare and contrast and then to draw conclusions. You need to continually relate the grid back to your class if you wish to retain a clear view of your direction. The *doing* of the grid was important because it blended the theory and the practical. It gave as an outcome a practical insight into relationships in a curriculum, in teaching and in learning.

The integration and sharing aspect caused a staff commonness to occur; a shared vision could arise from this.

It provided a crucial tool for analyzing literature. It allowed one to take a comment and to follow it through to see the full implications of what is said. The grid allows me to see beyond the obvious.

Group discussion was absolutely crucial. It provided a sounding board effect.

The interpretation [of the grids] allows you to draw out and internalize the obvious, to see previously unrelated points in your mind, and thus it is a mechanism for verifying one's educational stance. It gives your philosophy substance (a concreteness) and, therefore, evidence. You now can talk from a known and rational platform.

These comments are revealing and supportive. They emphasize the value of using repertory grids as part of the touchstone approach for promoting and enhancing critically reflective and increasingly intelligible discourse on teaching and learning. They highlight the efficacy of this approach in stimulating the critical exploration and deepening understanding by teachers of their personal theories of teaching. They stress the strength of the touchstone approach in developing a professional discourse on teaching and learning. But this strength will only be assured if some important potential difficulties are acknowledged and taken into account when using repertory grids in the touchstone approach. The teachers' comments were most helpful in identifying these potential difficulties and in suggesting ways in which their effects may be minimized.

A warning, perhaps pertinent to the use of any well-defined technique or sets of techniques, was sounded by the teacher who intimated that 'the technique may become more important than the issue'. That is, the emphasis must not be placed on the efficient use of the grids, and their techniques and routines for completion, but rather on what their use is able to tell us about teachers' personal theories of teaching. This difficulty can only be met if those who use the grids as part of the touchstone approach are made familiar with, and have a sound understanding of, the theoretical underpinnings of the development and use of repertory grids. For this reason, teachers must be prepared for the application of the touchstone approach by giving them a thorough grounding in its theoretical development, in particular, that relating to repertory grids, namely Kelly's theory of personal constructs. This grounding is an essential component of the touchstone approach to theory development.

Whilst this approach emphasizes the development of personal theories of teaching, a number of participants questioned whether the use of repertory grids in this approach allowed groups, rather than individuals, to explore issues deeply enough. This difficulty may need to be counteracted by ensuring that there is adequate time given to groups for sharing, reviewing, revising, and negotiating theories of teaching. That is, adequate time must be given to the negotiating phase of the process.

A critical aspect of the use of repertory grids is eliciting bipolar constructs. An important warning was given by one of the participants in suggesting that:

As the development of constructs is so vital perhaps more emphasis should be placed on these. It is very easy to develop constructs which are markedly bipolar in character, but, to me, this does not necessarily elicit subtle assumptions which we make in our teaching and learning. They therefore need to be developed in such a way that slight differences become visible at interpretation.

This comment draws attention to the need to help teachers move beyond constructs which are simplistic in the sense that they do not promote any increased depth or richness in the understanding of the complexities and subtleties of teaching and learning. Such constructs may deny the development of an initial discourse. What is required are constructs whose poles reveal subtle differences in meanings associated with teaching and learning. Such subtlety makes possible plausible alternative meanings, and hence personal theories of teaching. It makes feasible an open and critical debate about the appropriateness of the various alternatives as ways of describing effective teaching and learning. This critical dialogue can only occur in ways which will enrich the personal understanding of teaching and learning if alternative, plausible and subtlely insightful constructs are encouraged. The major encouragement for the touchstone approach comes through the theoretical input made to the program. For the teacher development program described in this book this input was made through a set of readings on curriculum development, specially written to highlight possible bipolar constructs.

In summary, the comments made by the participating teachers revealed the following advantages and disadvantages of the use of repertory grids to promote a critical dialogue in teaching as part of the touchstone approach to personal theory development.

i   It facilitated reflection on teaching practice and philosophies.

ii   It would be difficult to use with teachers in schools, because of the considerable time it requires.

iii   Repertory grids 'provide a systematic way of examining a number of problems' and 'are most successful in making us look at ourselves as teachers.'

iv   The idea of a model may have helped make the operation of the repertory grid more quickly understood.

v   The repertory grid 'gave a practical insight into the relationship between theory and classroom practice.'

vi   'The ordering of one's thinking is quite difficult without some sort of structure such as that provided by the grids.'

vii   The use of the grids did cause some initial discomfort to the participants, but in most cases this was overcome.

viii   The use of bipolar constructs forced consideration of alternatives.

ix   It 'forces the development of a new discourse or language so that teachers can converse, and, hopefully, reach agreement....'

x   The grids provide a means of uncovering the assumptions made regarding effective teaching and learning.

xi   '....the main points of one's thinking are succinctly revealed.'

xii   The grid 'enables me to clearly relate theories back to my actual personal educational beliefs and practices.'

xiii   'The technique can become more important than the issues.'

xiv   There was concern whether the use of repertory grids 'allowed us to get deeply enough into the issues as a group. It may have individually, but it would have been interesting to see how deep we would have gone as a group.'

xv   There were reservations about the application of repertory grids outside a 'theoretical environment'.

xvi   'It is very easy to develop constructs which are markedly bipolar in character, but ... this does not necessarily elicit subtle assumptions which we make in our teaching and learning.'

xvii The grids 'continually rechanneled thinking around the elements and constructs elicited, and focused the discourse back on the purposes it was meant to serve.'

xviii 'It has given a set of beliefs as to what I see as fundamental to me and my teaching.'

xix The grids provided a crucial tool for analyzing literature.

xx 'The grid provides a visual/concrete picture which is not abstract.'

As discussed above, the impact on the teacher development program of the reading program on approaches to curriculum development is vital. These readings were designed to highlight alternative perspectives of educating, teaching and learning, and to help participating teachers to express these alternative as bipolar constructs. In this way, as the teachers' understanding of the educational issues addressed by these readings increased, so did their capacity to develop more insightful and subtle constructs. By the enhanced use of such constructs in association with the development and interpretation of repertory grids a critical dialogue on educating, teaching and learning is developed. This will portray a deepening understanding of the dilemmas, richness, complexity and subtlety of our ways of describing effective teaching and learning; indeed, of our personal theories of teaching.

When asked about the helpfulness of the readings in developing constructs and the critical dialogue on teaching, teachers generally commented favourably. Perhaps the most fullsome comment was:

These exercises [readings] produced a feeling of fulfilment. The philosophical examination, mental exercise, heightened educational awareness, and the exposure to teaching and learning rationale, combined to provide a multidimensional stimulation for a teacher who felt that they had 'come in from the cold'. In our professional tune-up such comfortable bite sized bits were titillating apéritifs in our professional development menu, with the readings and the main course dish of repertory grids, although digestion took some time for some of the richer offerings. Eventually, one was left with a comfortably full feeling of satisfying contentment including surprisingly little indigestion.

Whilst all teachers were in agreement with these sentiments, most also wanted to add an important condition, namely, that the readings were only effective when they were used as a basis for discussions, either lecturer-led or within teacher groups. The following is typical of the comments expressing this view:

> The course readings were most intense, but through discussion within the group the wealth of knowledge, and richness of the material, became evident. However, without the group's support I may have found some of them difficult, to say the least. The group's effort in breaking them down into key issues, then constructs, was most helpful.

Similarly, lecturer-led discussion was considered helpful.

> I found both the lecturer's synthesis of the authors quoted and exercises of summarizing chapters from the readings, provided a valuable method of gaining a background for course discussions. I think all the groups appreciated not having to deal with masses of readings and texts that only remotely, or in parts, dealt with the focus of the question.

The purpose of the readings in raising an awareness of alternative educational perspectives was supported by the comments of the participants. As one stated: 'These readings allowed me to become aware that the various approaches to teaching and learning reflect various philosophical positions.'

Whilst almost all found the readings helpful, most admitted to initial difficulties and to the need for them to be discussed and interpreted. A typical response was:

> My initial reaction to the first set of readings, which were sent to me prior to the course, was that they were far above the actual plane on which I was operating and I could not relate them back to the teaching and learning situation. However, once the course began and the group, with the help of the lecturer, began to discuss the readings, I was able to pick out the relevant points and break them down for my own use.

In a similar manner another suggested that:

> At first glance, there were very heavy pieces of reading with no apparent usefulness. It took the group discussion and the repertory grids to help us get the necessary information from them.

But, I must admit as I progressed in this technique that I found the readings more enjoyable, and their meanings became more clear. As the meanings became clearer, I found that they were very closely related to teaching and learning and often expressed very important arguments currently being debated by teachers.

This initial sense of difficulty and frustration emphasizes the need to provide early and lecturer-supported discussions of any theoretical input. It also stresses the crucial importance of the teachers developing a dialogue which is both critical and clarifying, and hence of giving them both the theoretical and procedural bases for so doing. The touchstone approach provides such bases.

For the teachers, the readings:

i   allowed them to become aware that the various approaches to teaching and learning reflect differing philosophical positions;
ii stimulated ideas and knowledge that could be built on and used;
iii were initially difficult to understand;
iv required lecturer input and extensive group discussions for their clarifying and use in developing insights and stating these as bipolar constructs.

The readings did, with attention to the above, provide an excellent basis for the development of a critical dialogue on teaching and learning.

The touchstone approach seeks to enhance the intelligibility of teachers' descriptions of effective teaching and learning, and hence of their personal theories of teaching. One of the critical factors contributing to this intelligibility is whether such theories are practically plausible in the sense that they can be applied to actual instances of teaching and learning. To provide a basis for testing and monitoring any changes in this plausibility, teachers taking part in the teacher development program were asked to relate all their interpretations of the repertory grids they developed to a specific class, or group of students, which they were either currently teaching or had taught very recently. This class, or group, was referred to as the focus class.

All teachers were highly supportive of using a focus class, or similar notion, as a practical referent throughout the course. For example, one teacher was led to consider '. . . how meaningful much of this approach would have been without this personal point of reference. Unquestionably, it made the impacts and insights more dramatic, applying as they did in such a relevant, personal and even intimate way.'

Furthermore, and from the same teacher,

As difficult as it was at times to deal with the levels of abstraction covered by some of the readings, the focus class as a yard-stick was critical in ensuring that observations and findings made were somewhat near 'reality'. Besides 'keeping our feet on the ground' in this way during group and personal deliberations, the focus class provided a 'jumping off' point at times to provide another dimension to a discussion topic. Such 'concrete' experiences provided by the focus classes of the course members, by permeating our deliberations, made a significant contribution to the 'applicability' of our conclusions.

Continuing reference to the focus class enhanced the practical plausibility of statements relating to teaching and learning for this class. That is, the practical plausibility of the teacher's personal theories of teaching was enhanced.

Other comments serve to reinforce this position.

The idea of a focus class was excellent. As teachers are basically concerned with teaching and learning, and as this occurs everyday in our various classes, then we need to focus on these classes. Constant images of students, and your reactions with them, come into your mind, and you constantly test the theories and ideas in this practical (but visualized) situation. Perhaps more pre-course time should be spent on clarifying the focus class so that it, as a reference point, becomes very fixed.

Another teacher commented:

This is a valuable idea as it prevents me from becoming embedded in theories, and brings one's reflections back to the level of what I am going to do to enhance the effectiveness of my teaching-learning situation, which I encounter daily, rather than on the plane of an all-embracing educational philosophy to be 'kept in the head', but not put into practice. Therefore, when a repertory grid is completed for a particular reading, one ends up with a set of guidelines for effective teaching and learning with your own focus class or classes.

Others commented that reference to a focus class made them think more specifically about how to adjust teaching strategies, curriculum content and pupil expectations for effective teaching and learning for the focus class. In the words of one participant, it 'made me talk in specifics and not to generalize. It gave my thinking a human perspective — is not this what teaching is all about?'

In summary, the teachers saw the following advantages and disadvantages of the idea of a focus class.

    i   The idea of a focus class formed an important basis for the program.

    ii   The focus class was an advantage 'when you had to consider some specific situations and practices with regard to a class, rather than creating a hypothetical situation.'

    iii   'Unquestionably, it [the focus class] made the impacts and insights more dramatic, applying as they did in such a relevant, personal and even intimate way.'

    iv   'As difficult as it was at times to deal with the levels of abstraction covered by some of the readings, the focus class, as a yard-stick, was critical in ensuring that observations and findings were made "somewhat near reality".'

    v   'Such "concrete" experiences provided by the focus classes of the course members, by permeating our deliberations, made a significant contribution to the "applicability" of our conclusions.'

    vi   'Constant images of students, and your reactions with them, come into your mind, and you constantly test theories and ideas in this practical (but visualized) situation.'

    vii   In this program 'a low-key, although always present, approach was used' in emphasizing the use of the focus class.

    viii   A clear idea of the type of focus class most suitable to the program may need to be given to participants prior to the commencement of the program.

    ix   'The focus class has made me think *specifically* about how I adjust my (a) method, (b) content, and (c) expectations to a particular class.' These readings allowed me to become aware that the various approaches to teaching and learning reflect various philosophical positions.

The basis for assessing a teacher's progress throughout the teacher development program was the keeping of a professional journal. In this journal teachers kept detailed records and evaluations of all work undertaken during the program. This included full details of the development, analysis and interpretations of repertory grids during, and at the conclusion of, the program. No other form of assessment was required.

The participating teachers were unanimous in their support for this approach. One of the more insightful, supportive comments made was:

> Because the theme of the course was to question their own values and attitudes towards education, I believe the approach taken to the assessment of the course was particularly appropriate because students were assessed from the aspect of where they had reached as an individual with regard to teaching and learning as it related to their focus class.

In further support for the approach several teachers emphasized the centrality of self-evaluation in teacher development. As one said,

> I feel the real assessment has been a constant self-evaluation as no comment or statement has been made without further reflection and modification. The materials written have also helped in self-assessment as each final grid interpretation has a review and test of what was learned. Thus, it soon became obvious if you had completed enough work and at enough depth. This piece of writing now being completed also indicates the self-assessment program. How can you review a course if you have not learned anything or taken part at some depth in the various discussions?

Whilst there was overwhelming support for assessment using a professional journal, some teachers expressed some initial reservations. These are encapsulated in the quotations which follow, both of which have evident and important implications for monitoring and assessing teacher development.

First,

> The difficulty I had at the beginning of the course was to establish clearly in my mind how this related to the quality and quantity of what I was expected to present.

> This is obviously a legacy of my experiences over the years with assessment requirements that have laid down exams, essays, oral components, etc. Once one comes to terms with the idea of a professional journal as the major assessment method, there is no difficulty in seeing this as a means of assessment.

Second, and with more insight,

The assesssing by course work, exercises, and the professional journal was different to approaches that I had previously experienced. Initially, I found it difficult to accept because not having assignments meant I did not really know how I was going in the 'eyes of others'. To have an assessment resting on an 'unknown' is a difficult concept to initially accept because people in these courses are primarily completing qualifications and therefore are continually conscious of how they are going. Once I 'came to grips' with this, I found this style of assessment a real innovation. To actually be assessed on course work is refreshing and to incorporate the completing of a professional journal into this assessment meant that:

a   you had to become organized;
b   you readily knew where things were;
c   you were therefore more effective personally in your teaching and in your dealings with staff and the community.

The real bonus of this form of assessment is the legacy of the professional journal exercise and the fact that it is so very relevant. Thus, to me, this was of real personal worth.

In summary, the comments on the use of the professional journal for assessment were as follows.

i   The 'student-centred' approach to assessment was strongly supported.
ii   The use of the professional journal could have been supplemented with individual student discussions with the lecturer in charge.
iii   The assessment approach was 'contextually appropriate, coherent and enlightened'.
iv   There were some difficulties for participants in knowing how the professional journal related to the quality and quantity of what was expected of them.
v   Assessment using the journal was complemented by observation by the lecturer of the development of participants during the program.
vi   The assessment procedure was 'more generally meaningful as it focuses on self-evaluation....'
vii   The materials written helped in self-assessment as each grid interpretation was 'a review and test of what was learned'.

viii 'As much of our student assessment is continuous and based on what is achieved in the classroom, this is only proper for teachers to undergo the same process.'

ix Combination of the repertory grid exercises and the journal was seen as a fair method of assessment.

x The assessment approach 'presupposes that the purpose of the course is to enable the student to develop his or her skills and ideas in the areas of teaching and learning.'

Finally, what modifications to the approach were suggested? Those suggested were:

i Some additional tutorial sessions may have been helpful.

ii Time constraints had some limiting effects, such as on-time for individual study and writing.

iii A model of a repertory grid, its analysis and interpretation, should be provided at the beginning of the course.

iv Regularizing the periods of time between the three periods of the program may be beneficial.

v The timing of changes in the membership of groups needs further consideration.

vi The repertory grid approach may need to be modified to make it more appropriate for use by teachers in schools.

vii A more detailed introduction of each member to the class may facilitate later discussions.

viii Procedures for indicating participant progress during the course may need to be developed.

Each of the changes suggested can be readily incorporated in future programs, and can be further evaluated. None of these changes would have any detrimental effect on the theoretical and procedural bases developed for the touchstone approach.

To conclude the evaluation of the teacher development program, each participant was asked to speculate on the personal long-term effects of having participated in this program. The participants saw these as follows:

i a greater awareness of alternative philosophical positions and practical approaches to teaching and learning;

ii a greater concentration on the 'skills of negotiation' of teachers in the development of curricula;

iii encouragement of long-term professional growth;

Table 5.1. Evaluation of the Meeting of Program Purposes

Individual purposes	
Developing each participant's capacity to	
i recognize and describe;	27
ii explore;	27
iii review;	28
iv revise and clarify	29

alternative frames of reference which they may use to describe effective teaching and learning.

Group purposes	
Developing each participant's capacity to	
i communicate;	23
ii share;	20
iii negotiate	21

these frames of reference with other program participants.

   iv   an increased awareness of the need to relate theory to classroom practice;

   v   an increased awareness of the need to approach teacher development tasks through working with individual teachers, and of basing these developments on teaching and learning;

   vi   an increase in skills in articulating the constructs being used to describe teaching and learning;

   vii   a positive attitude to student-centred and student-negotiated curricula;

   viii   an increased capacity to see the bases from which others are arguing in relation to teaching and learning;

   ix   an increased critical capacity when reading literature on education;

   x   a reduction in the gap between theories of effective teaching and learning and classroom practice;

   xi   a greater awareness of the 'difficulties, complexities and intricacies of the curriculum';

   xii   the clarification of personal educational philosophies;

   xiii   a greater confidence to act in a 'negotiated environment';

   xiv   the provision of the 'management and development tool' of repertory grids 'allows one to work through a task in an intelligent and logical manner.'

In completing the evaluation of the touchstone approach in terms of meeting individual and group purposes each participant's responses to each of the evaluation questions given at the beginning of the chapter was considered. The responses for each question were summarized and assessed in terms of whether or not they indicated achievement of the individual and/or group purposes of the program. Table 5.1 shows this analysis, with the number for each purpose indicating the number of occasions on which teacher responses indicated the achievement of this purpose.

This analysis shows that all four individual purposes were very strongly supported by the comments of the participants. Thus the teacher development program was effective in assisting participants in developing capacities to recognize, describe, review, revise and clarify alternative frames of reference, which they may use in describing effective teaching and learning. The group purposes are strongly supported, but slightly less so than the individual purposes. Nevertheless, the comments of the participants indicate that the program was effective in developing their expertise to communicate, share and negotiate frames of reference for use in describing effective teaching and learning.

Thus the touchstone approach to teacher development was very effective in meeting these individual and group purposes, and, therefore, in developing a critically effective dialogue on teaching and learning and hence on the teachers' personal theories of teaching and learning.

Chapter 6

Evaluation of the Effectiveness of the Touchstone Approach

At particular stages in this teacher development program each participating senior teacher developed, analyzed and interpreted a repertory grid based on descriptions of effective teaching and learning for their focus class. This chapter reports a detailed study of these analyses and interpretation as undertaken by each of three teachers. These three case studies use the repertory grid procedures, as described in Chapter 2, to monitor and assess changes in the intelligibility of the descriptions of effective teaching and learning during the program for these teachers. The effectiveness of the touchstone approach in enhancing descriptive intelligibility for each of the three teachers is then discussed.

The teacher development program was conducted in three periods, each of one week. At the end of each of these periods, each teacher completed a repertory grid on describing effective teaching and learning for their focus class. Correlation matrices for both elements and bipolar statements (constructs) were completed. Each teacher analyzed and interpreted these matrices and the repertory grid in terms of describing effective teaching and learning for their focus class. The three repertory grids considered in each of the case studies are called Repertory Grid 1, Repertory Grid 2 and Repertory Grid 3 in the order of their completion during the program.

Each of the case studies includes the following:

a a summary of the qualifications and teaching experience of the teacher;
b a brief description of the focus class;
c Repertory Grid 1, including:
   i elements of the grid;
   ii bipolar statements (constructs) of the grid;
   iii the completed repertory grid;

    iv correlation matrices for elements and bipolar statements;

    v calculation of coefficients of consistency and plausibility;

    vi interpretation of correlation matrices' co-referencing of elements and coefficients of consistency and plausibility;

  d Repertory Grid 2, including:

    i elements of the grid;

    ii bipolar statements (constructs) of the grid;

    iii the completed repertory grid;

    iv correlation matrices for elements and bipolar statements;

    v calculation of the coefficients of consistency and plausibility;

    vi interpretation of correlation matrices, co-referencing of elements and coefficients of consistency and plausibility;

  e Repertory Grid 3, including:

    i elements of the grid;

    ii bipolar statements (constructs) of the grid;

    iii the completed repertory grid;

    iv correlation matrices for elements and bipolar statements;

    v calculation of the coefficients of consistency and plausibility;

    vi interpretation of correlation matrices, co-referencing of elements, and coefficients of consistency and plausibility.

  f a discussion of the changes, throughout the program, in the description of effective teaching and learning for the focus class, particularly as these relate to changes in the coefficients of consistency and plausibility, the co-referencing of elements, and to the teachers' interpretations of their repertory grids.

All sixteen teachers who began the program completed it. The following areas of education were represented by these teachers:

technical and further education (including nurse education)	(3 teachers)
secondary education (grades 7–10)	(8 teachers)
primary education (grades K-6)	(5 teachers)

One teacher was selected from each of three areas for the case studies. This selection was made on the basis that the approach to teacher development of this program should be equally applicable to participants from any area of education and professional background, and that this applicability was best illustrated by selecting teachers from as wide a range of backgrounds, and current responsibilities, as possible. The three participants selected were from the three broad areas of education represented in the program — primary, secondary and further education. The primary teacher, John, is a vice-principal of a large primary school in a predominantly economically and socially deprived area; the secondary teacher is a senior master in a large district high school in a relatively prosperous and educationally conscious rural area; and the further education representative is a senior nurse educator in a large metropolitan hospital.

Case Study A (Secondary Education)

John is a senior master of English and social sciences in a large district high school, which serves a prosperous farming district. Twelve years of teaching have been completed, with the last four as a senior master responsible for English and social sciences. John's initial period of four years of training included the completion of the degree of Bachelor of Arts and a Diploma of Education. An emerging interest and strengthening influence for John is the teaching of English, particularly reading, to primary school children.

The focus class selected by John was a grade 9 English class at the district high school. The class had an enrolment of twenty-four students, including three students who lacked motivation, one of whom was a severe behaviour problem. The remaining students were very highly motivated. The class included a mixture of average and above-average ability students.

Repertory Grid 1

At the end of the first week of the program John used his set of statements of the conditions for effective teaching and learning for his focus class to develop, analyze and interpret a repertory grid.

Elements of the Grid

The elements developed by John were as follows:

Element   Statement of element
  A   Good teaching provides students with the opportunity to
          measure their progress.

B   Good teaching involves individual and group work equally.

C   Good teaching involves communicating in a manner suitable for the maturity level of the child.

D   Good teaching involves negotiation of the curriculum with the students.

E   Good teaching encourages the development of self-motivation.

F   Good teaching draws on a wide range of experiences and resources.

Constructs (Bipolar Statements)

Using the triad method, John elicited the following bipolar statements from the above set of elements:

Construct	Initial pole	Emergent pole
1	Learners should be assured of success.	Learners should be able to cope with failure
2	Learning relies on student motivation.	Learner relies on teacher motivation.
3	Learning best occurs when curriculum is interrelated.	Learning best occurs when the curriculum is subject oriented.
4	Students learn best when the method is negotiated.	Students learn best when teaching method is determined for them.
5	Learning occurs best when student interests and needs are met.	Learning occurs best when society's needs are met.
6	A rich learning environment results when a wide range of resources is utilized.	A rich learning environment is teacher-dependent.

Completion of the Repertory Grid

Using the procedure described in Chapter 2, John completed the repertory grid as shown in Table 6.1.

Table 6.1. Repertory Grid 1

Construct	Elements						Construct
Initial pole	A	B	C	D	E	F	Emergent pole
C1P1	√	√	√	√	√	√	C1P2
C2P1	√	√	X	√	√	√	C2P2
C3P1	√	√	√	√	√	√	C3P2
C4P1	√	X	√	√	√	√	C4P2
C5P1	√	X	√	√	√	√	C5P2
C6P1	√	√	√	√	√	√	C6P2

Table 6.2. Correlation Matrix for Elements

Elements	A	B	C	D	E	F
A		4	5	6	6	6
B			3	4	4	4
C				5	5	5
D					6	6
E						6
F						

Table 6.3. Correlation Matrix for Constructs

Construct	1	2	3	4	5	6
1		5	6	5	5	6
2			5	4	4	5
3				5	5	6
4					6	5
5						5
6						

Correlation Matrices for Elements and Constructs

Using the procedures described in Chapter 2, the correlation matrices for both the elements and the constructs were completed in Tables 6.2 and 6.3 respectively.

Calculation of Coefficients of Consistency and Plausibility

These were calculated by John as described in Chapter 2.

Coefficient of consistency. For a repertory grid of n elements and m bipolar statements, the coefficient of consistency

$$= \frac{2 \text{ (sum of element corr. scores)}}{mn(n-1)}$$

In this case n = 6 and m = 6, and the sum of the element correlation scores is 75.

Hence coefficient of consistency

$$= \frac{2 \times 75}{6^2 (6-1)}$$

$$= \underline{0.83}$$

Coefficient of plausibility. The coefficient of plausibility = Sum of adjusted construct corr. score from median score (number of pairs of constructs × maximum difference score).

For a grid with six elements, the median construct correlation score is 3. If the correlation scores are adjusted to differences from this median score, the adjusted correlation matrix is as shown in Table 6.4.

Interpretation of the Repertory Grid and the Correlation Matrices

Coherence of elements. The elements of the repertory grid give a description of effective teaching and learning for the focus class of the participant. As discussed in Chapter 1, the coherence of such a set of statements may be considered in terms of the co-referencing of the constituent semantic units of the description, that is, in terms of the elements of the description. If explicit co-referencing occurs, the referents of each element should coincide with the referents of at least one other element. For the above grid, the referents contained within the various elements are as in Table 6.5.

All elements, except F, contain a reference to students. Hence elements A to E can be linked through their reference to students. They each describe conditions supporting a student-centred approach to teaching

Table 6.4. Adjusted Correlation Matrix

Construct	1	2	3	4	5	6
1		2	3	2	2	3
2			2	1	1	2
3				2	2	3
4					3	2
5						2
6						

Table 6.5. Referents for the Elements

Element	First referent	Second referent
A	Student(s)	Progress
B	Individuals and groups	Work
C	Manner of communicating	Maturity level of child
D	Curriculum	Students
E	Self (student)	Motivation
F	Experiences and resources	Range

and learning. By referring to groups as well as individuals, and suggesting equal individual and group work, element B specifies a condition only partly supportive of a student-centred approach. Elements A, C, D and E would be expected, therefore, to correlate strongly. Element B would be expected to correlate less strongly with this set of elements. An examination of the correlation matrix for the elements shows that the correlation scores are lower for element B than any other element.

In discussing the correlation scores, the teacher concerned made the following comments:

Correlating elements	Correlation score	Teacher's comments
A and D	6/6	This emphasizes that a negotiated learning environment will enable rapid student progress.
A and E	6/6	This emphasizes that the more self-motivated the

		student, the greater the progress.
D and E	6/6	A negotiated curriculum results in highly self-motivated students.

These comments suggest first, that effective teaching and learning is being perceived by John as student-centred. Second, John sees a negotiated learning environment as being linked with student progress, which, in turn, is linked with student self-motivation, which is seen to result from a negotiated curriculum. Thus a negotiated learning environment, student progress, negotiated curricula and student self-motivation are explicitly co-referenced. In terms of co-referencing, elements A, D and E formed, for John, a highly consistent description of effective teaching and learning.

The final element F refers to the provision of a wide range of resources and experiences. As resources and experiences are not referred to in any other elements, element F does not explicitly co-refer to any other elements. The correlation matrix indicates, however, that it is highly correlated (correlation score of 6/6) with elements A, D and E. John made the following comments on these high correlations:

Correlating elements	Correlation score	John's comments
A and F	6/6	This emphasizes that the wider the range of experiences, the greater the student progress.
D and F	6/6	A negotiated curriculum will result in a greater range of experiences for the learner.
E and F	6/6	A wide range of experiences will result in the self-motivation of the students.

These comments suggest that John perceived the provision of a wide range of experiences as being linked to student progress, negotiated curricula and student self-motivation. These links of A, D and E with F are, for John, implicit within the description of effective teaching and learning given by the elements of the grid. Thus elements A, D and E are coherent in terms of explicit co-referencing with one another, and all are coherent, implicitly, with element F. Element C, which has correlation scores of 5/6 with each of elements A, D, E and F, co-refers explicitly to A, D and E through its reference to the child or student. Although John did not comment on the high correlations of elements C and F, a link between the provision of 'a wide range of experiences and resources' and 'communicating in a manner suitable to the maturity level of the child' seems to have been assumed.

Elements B and C have a low correlation score (3/6). For John, this appeared to result from a conflict between communicating according to the maturity level of the child and students working in groups. Whilst the notion of group work conflicts with all other elements of the grid, for John this conflict seems to be highlighted by reference to maturity levels suitable for individual children.

Thus for John's description of the conditions for effective teaching and learning

i   elements A, D and E show explicit co-reference;
ii   element F is implicitly related to elements A, D and E;
iii element C co-refers, implicitly, to elements, A, D and E, but at a lower level;
iv   element B has a low degree of correlation with the other elements.

Coefficient of consistency.   These coefficients indicate the overall degree of correlation between elements within a grid. This degree of correlation is a measure of the consistency of the elements in describing effective teaching and learning.

The coefficients of consistency for the various groups of elements considered above in i–iv are:

i	A, D and E	1.0
ii	A, D, E and F	1.0
iii	A, C, D, E and F	0.93
iv	A, B, C, D, E and F	0.83

The high degree of consistency of the elements of this grid, and the explicit co-referencing between elements A, D and E, suggest a highly coherent description of effective teaching and learning using these elements. The inclusion of element F, which correlates implicitly with elements A, D and E, gives a group of elements which give, for John, a fully consistent description of effective teaching and learning.

Plausibility of Descriptions of Effective Teaching and Learning

The pairs of constructs with high (6/6) correlation scores are:

> constructs 1 and 3
> constructs 1 and 6
> constructs 3 and 6
> constructs 4 and 5

Constructs 1, 3 and 6 were considered by John as a group. An examination of the completed repertory grid showed that the correlation of constructs 1, 3 and 6 is between their initial poles. Hence the description of effective teaching and learning, given by the elements of the grid, was interpreted by John to mean, in part, that:

> learners should be assured of success (Initial pole, Construct 1);

> learning best occurs when the curriculum is interrelated (Initial pole, Construct 2);

> a rich learning environment results when a wide range of resources is utilized (Initial pole, Construct 6).

Similarly, the high correlation of constructs 4 and 5 refers to the initial poles of these constructs. These are:

> students learn best when the teaching method is negotiated (Initial pole, Construct 4);

> learning occurs best when student interests and needs are met (Initial pole, Construct 5).

A further examination of the repertory grid revealed that the sets of constructs 1, 3 and 6, and constructs 4 and 5, do not correlate perfectly because of their different matchings with element B. Whereas element B is matched with the initial poles of constructs 1, 3 and 6, it is matched with the emergent poles of constructs 4 and 5. It is this latter matching which has substantially reduced the correlation of the constructs.

For John's focus class, 'Good teaching involves individual and group work equally' was matched with 'Students learn best when the teaching method is determined for them' and 'Learning occurs best when society's needs are met.' That is, equating individual and group work has been interpreted by John to mean that the teaching method must be determined by the teacher, and that the curriculum should be based upon the needs of society. Both interpretations indicate reservations by John in his support for a student-centred approach to teaching and learning. These same reservations were revealed in the discussion of the correlation matrix for the elements.

In addition, element C has been matched with the emergent pole of construct 2. That is, 'Good teaching involves communicating in a manner suitable for the maturity level for the child' is matched with 'Learning relies on teacher motivation.' This matching may indicate John's reluctance to relinquish a view of teaching in which student learning is teacher motivated and directed. If element B is eliminated from the repertory grid, then the plausibility coefficient becomes 0.83. If elements B and C are eliminated, the plausibility coefficient becomes 1.0. These coefficients reflect the comments made above. Thus the most plausible description of effective teaching and learning for the focus class results from a grid containing elements A, D, E and F.

In summary, by including element B, and to a lesser extent element C, there is a loss in coherence of the description of effective teaching and learning provided by the elements of the grid and a substantial loss in the plausibility of the description based on these elements. This analysis may also indicate, as discussed above, difficulties for John in describing a student-centred approach to teaching and learning.

Repertory Grid 2

This grid, and its analysis and interpretation, was completed by John at the end of the second week of the teacher development program.

Elements of the Grid

John suggested the following conditions for effective teaching and learning for his focus class.

Element	Statement of element
A	Effective learning/teaching best occurs when the curriculum is negotiated.
B	Effective learning/teaching best occurs when teachers are aware of individual student capabilities and social backgrounds.

C   Effective learning/teaching best occurs when teachers are self-motivated.
D   Effective learning/teaching best occurs when the teacher is a facilitator.
E   Effective learning/teaching best occurs when a wide range of resources is drawn on.
F   Effective learning/teaching best occurs when short-term goals are present.
G   Effective teaching/learning occurs when individualized assessment occurs.
H   Effective teaching/learning involves communicating in a manner suitable to the stage of the child.
I   Effective learning requires a secure environment.
J   Learning occurs best when the curriculum is interrelated.

Constructs (Bipolar Statements)

Using the triad method, John elicited the following bipolar constructs from this set of elements.

Construct	Initial pole	Emergent pole
1	A negotiated curriculum for individual student needs and capabilities.	Consideration of the students' background allows appropriate student learning.
2	The 'teacher-facilitator' ensures that students learn as individuals.	The teacher as expert emphasizes content.
3	Self-motivated students require a wide range of resources.	Self-motivated students use the teacher as facilitator.
4	To achieve short-term goals a range of resources is required.	Individualized assessment requires short-term goals.
5	Individualized assessment considers the stage the child is at.	Short-term goals allow the child to move stages more quickly.
6	A secure environment facilitates the child's development.	A child's education is based on communication.

| 7 | An interrelated curriculum provides a secure environment. | Communication provides a secure environment. |

Completion of the Repertory Grid

John then completed his second repertory grid using these elements and constructs. This is shown in Table 6.6.

Correlation Matrices for Elements and Constructs

Using the same procedures as before, John completed correlation matrices for both elements and constructs. These are shown in Tables 6.7 and 6.8. The adjusted construct correlation matrix is shown in Table 6.9.

Calculation of Coefficients of Coherence and Plausibility

This enabled John to calculate the coefficients of consistency and plausibility for this grid. These were found to be 0.59 and 0.24 respectively.

Interpretation of the Correlation Matrices

Correlation of elements. The referents included in the elements were as follows:

Elements		Referents	
A	Curriculum		
B	Teachers	Industrial student	Social backgrounds
C	Students	Self-motivation	—
D	Teacher	Facilitator	—
E	Resources	—	—
F	Goals		
G	Individualized assessment		
H	Communicating	Stage of the child	
I	Environment		
J	Curriculum		

Table 6.6. Repertory Grid 2

Construct	Elements										Construct
Initial pole	A	B	C	D	E	F	G	H	I	J	Emergent pole
C1P1	√	X	√	√	√	√	√	√	√	√	C1P2
C2P1	√	√	√	√	√	√	√	√	√	X	C2P2
C3P1	√	√	X	X	√	√	X	X	X	√	C3P2
C4P1	X	√	√	√	√	X	√	√	√	X	C4P2
C5P1	X	√	X	X	X	√	√	√	√	X	C5P2
C6P1	X	√	√	√	X	√	√	X	√	√	C6P2
C7P1		X	√	√	√	√	√	X	√	√	C7P2

Table 6.7. Correlation Matrix for Elements

Element	A	B	C	D	E	F	G	H	I	J
A		2	4	4	6	6	4	3	4	4
B			3	3	3	3	3	4	3	3
C				7	5	5	5	4	5	5
D					5	5	5	4	5	5
E						5	3	4	3	5
F							5	2	5	5
G								4	7	3
H									4	2
I										3
J										

Given these referents, only limited explicit co-referencing can occur between the elements. In particular, elements E, F, G and I each have single referents, which are not included in the referents for any other element. Explicit co-referencing occurs between elements A and J and elements B, C, D and H.

The correlation scores for the possible pairs of elements drawn from these two sets of elements are:

Table 6.8. Correlation Matrix for Constructs

Construct	1	2	3	4	5	6	7
1		8	4	5	3	6	9
2			4	5	5	6	7
3				5	3	4	5
4					4	5	4
5						5	2
6							7

Table 6.9. Adjusted Construct Correlation Matrix

Construct	1	2	3	4	5	6	7
1		3	1	0	2	1	4
2			1	0	0	1	2
3				0	2	1	0
4					1	0	1
5						0	3
6							2

Pair of elements	Correlation score (maximum 10)
A, J	4
B, C	3
B, D	3
B, H	4
C, D	7
C, H	4
D, H	4

Of these, only elements C and D show a high correlation. Thus for John and his focus class, 'Effective learning/teaching best occurs when students are self-motivated' was highly correlated with 'Effective learning/ teaching best occurs when the teacher is a facilitator.' That is, the self-motivation of students was associated, implicitly, with the teacher facilitating, rather than motivating, student learning.

Elements G and I also have a maximum correlation score of 7. That is, 'Effective learning/teaching occurs when individualized assessment occurs' was linked with 'Effective learning requires a secure environment.' This is an implicit link, the implication being that there is a necessary relationship between 'individualized assessment' and 'secure environment'. Both pairs of elements A and E, and A and F have correlation scores of 6. Thus for John, 'Effective learning best occurs when the curriculum is negotiated' may be implicitly related to 'Effective learning/teaching best occurs when a wide range of resources is drawn on' and 'Effective learning/teaching best occurs when short-term goals are present.'

For John, there is an implied link between 'negotiating' the curriculum, a 'wide range' of resources and 'short-term' goals. What seems to be suggested by this link is that an essential requirement for effective teaching and learning, when the curriculum is negotiated with students, is that short-term goals are negotiated and fixed. When this is done, the more individualized nature of the curriculum being taught, to allow these short-term goals to be met, will require the provision of a wide range of resources. This interpretation is crucial to John's understanding of effective teaching with his focus class.

If the repertory grid is restricted to elements C, D, G and I, then the coefficient of consistency = 0.83 and the coefficient of plausibility = 0.62. An inspection of the correlation matrix shows that the correlation scores for element B are less than, or equal to, 3. If element B is eliminated from the grid, then the coefficient of consistency = 0.63 and the coefficient of plausibility = 0.32. If, in addition, element H is removed from the grid, as it has low correlation scores, then the coefficient of consistency = 0.64 and the coefficient of plausibility = 0.36. Thus the removal of elements B and H from the grid changes the coefficients of consistency and plausibility only marginally (by 0.05 and 0.12 respectively). Only the grid containing elements C, D, G and I has higher coefficients of consistency (0.84) and plausibility (0.62). These compare with 0.59 and 0.24 respectively for Repertory Grid 1.

Repertory Grid 2 has ten elements. A core set of elements, C, D, G and I, is highly consistent, whilst the full grid has very low consistency and plausibility and limited co-referencing. This indicates that the elements, other than C, D, G and I, do not assist in giving a coherent and plausible description of effective teaching and learning, These elements have introduced additional factors, such as short-term goals and a secure environment, which John was unable to integrate into an intelligible description of effective teaching and learning at this stage of the program. That is, the program has raised John's awareness of these factors, but he has not been able to interrelate them intelligibly with the core elements C, D, G and I of the grid.

Plausibility of constructs. An examination of the repertory grid and the adjusted correlation matrix for constructs indicates that the following pairs of construct poles are highly correlated:

Pairs of construct poles	Correlation score
C1P1–C7P1	9
CIP2–C7P2	9
C5P2–C7P1	2
C5P1–C7P2	2
C1P1–C2P1	8
C1P2–C2P2	8
C1P2–C5P1	3
C1P1–C5P2	3
C3P1–C5P2	3
C3P2–C5P1	3

These constructs can be linked, using the above pairings, to form the following sets of linked statements:

(a)   C2P1–C1P1–C7P1–C5P2–C3P1
(b)   C2P2–C1P2–C7P2–C5P1–C3P2

Set (a) forms the initial poles and set (b) the emergent poles of a revised repertory grid.

Furthermore, constructs 4 and 6 would not be included in this grid as their poles do not discriminate the meanings of the elements of the original repertory grid. The revised constructs are shown in Table 6.10.

For John, these two sets of statements represented two contrasting interpretations of effective teaching and learning. John interpreted the description of effective teaching and learning, given as elements of the repertory grid, as meaning the statements of the initial poles of the revised set of constructs.

If this revised set of constructs is used with elements C, D, G and I, as argued in the preceding section, the repertory grid is as shown in Table 6.11, and the correlation matrices as in Tables 6.12 and 6.13.

Table 6.10. *Revised Set of Constructs*

Construct pole	Initial pole	Emergent pole	Construct
C2P1	The 'teacher facilitator' ensures that students learn as individuals	The teacher as expert emphasizes content	C2P2
C1P1	A negotiated curriculum caters for individual student needs and capabilities	Consideration of the students' background allows appropriate student learning	C1P2
C7P1	An interrelated curriculum provides a secure environment	Communication provides a secure environment	C7P2
C5P2	Short-term goals allow the child to move stages more quickly	Individualized assessment considers the stage the child is at	C5P1
C3P1	Self-motivated students require a wide range of resources	Self-motivated students use the teacher as facilitator	C3P2

Table 6.11. *Revised Repertory Grid*

Construct	Elements				Construct
Initial pole	C	D	G	I	Emergent pole
C2P1					C2P2
C1P1					C1P2
C7P1					C7P2
C5P2					C5P1
C3P2					C3P1

Table 6.12. *Correlation Matrix for Elements*

Element	C	D	G	I
C		5	4	4
D			4	4
G				4
I				

Table 6.13. Correlation Matrix for Constructs

Construct	1	2	3	4	5
C2P1		5	4	4	5
C1P1			5	4	5
C7P1				4	5
C5P2					4
C3P2					

Table 6.14. Adjusted Construct Correlation Matrix

Construct	C2P1	C1P1	C7P1	C5P2	C3P2
C2P1		2	1	1	2
C1P1			2	1	2
C7P1				1	2
C5P2					1
C3P2					

Table 6.15. Revised Repertory Grid

	C	D	G	I	
C2P1	✓	✓	✓	✓	C2P2
C1P1	✓	✓	✓	✓	C1P2
C7P1	✓	✓	✓	✓	C7P2
C5P2	✓	✓	✓	✓	C5P1
C3P2	✓	✓	✓	✓	C3P1

The median construct scores are 2 and 3, and hence the adjusted construct correlation matrix is as in Table 6.14, and has a coefficient of plausibility of 0.75. The adjustment of the constructs, as above, has increased the plausibility of the description provided by elements C, D, G and I from 0.62 to 0.75. Thus the most consistent and plausible description of effective teaching available from Repertory Grid 2 is given by the revised grid shown as Table 6.15.

Repertory Grid 3

This grid, and its analysis and interpretation, was completed by John at the end of the final week of the teacher development program.

Elements of the Grid

John stated the conditions for effective teaching and learning for the focus class as the following elements.

Element	Statement of element
A	The role of language is crucial in achieving effective learning.
B	The curriculum should be process oriented to enable effective teaching and learning.
C	Effective teaching and learning should emanate from a core curriculum.
D	Effective teaching and learning involves a holistic view of the child's education.
E	Effective learning and teaching involves student input.
F	Assessment is an integral part of individualized curriculum.
G	Effective teaching and learning occurs when the child, rather than the teacher, is the centre of the learning process.
H	Effective learning and teaching occurs when there is a negotiated view of the world.

Constructs (Bipolar Statements)

Using the triad method, John elicited the following set of bipolar statements from these elements.

Construct	Initial pole	Emergent pole
1	Language must be plausible.	Knowledge speaks for itself.
2	A curriculum should emphasize experiences.	A curriculum should emphasize outcomes.

3	Effective teaching and learning will be based on agreed values.	Effective teaching and learning will be subject-based.
4	Effective teaching and learning needs to be coherent and contextual.	Effective teaching and learning needs to be consistent and universal.
5	Effective teaching and learning occurs when there is student input.	Effective teaching and learning occurs when learning is prescriptive.
6	Assessment should be individualized.	Assessment should be standardized.
7	Teaching should be child-centred.	The teacher directs the learning.
8	Effective learning and teaching occurs when there is a negotiated view of the world.	Effective learning and teaching occurs when the view of the world is set.

Completion of the Repertory Grid

John then completed the repertory grid as shown in Table 6.16.

Correlation Matrices for Elements and Constructs

Correlation matrices for both elements and constructs were then completed as before. These are shown as Tables 6.17 and 6.18. The adjusted correlation matrix for constructs is shown as Table 6.19.

Calculation of Coefficients of Consistency and Plausibility

These were calculated to be 0.84 and 0.86 respectively.

If element C is eliminated from the grid, because of its low correlation, the coefficient of consistency is 1.0 and the coefficient of plausibility is 1.0. That is, the grid consisting of elements A, B, D, E, F, G and H is fully consistent and plausible. This indicates that for John and his focus class the notion of core curriculum, as in element C, is neither consistent nor plausible with the other elements of the grid.

Table 6.16. Repertory Grid 3

Construct	Elements								Construct
Initial pole	A	B	C	D	E	F	G	H	Emergent pole
C1P1	✓	✓	X	✓	✓	✓	✓	✓	C1P2
C2P1	✓	✓	✓	✓	✓	✓	✓	✓	C2P2
C3P1	✓	✓	✓	✓	✓	✓	✓	✓	C3P2
C4P1	✓	✓	✓	✓	✓	✓	✓	✓	C4P2
C5P1	✓	✓	X	✓	✓	✓	✓	✓	C5P2
C6P1	✓	✓	X	✓	✓	✓	✓	✓	C6P2
C7P1	✓	✓	X	✓	✓	✓	✓	✓	C7P2
C8P1	✓	✓	X	✓	✓	✓	✓	✓	C8P2

Table 6.17. Correlation Matrix for Elements

Elements	A	B	C	D	E	F	G	H
A		8	3	8	8	8	8	8
B			3	8	8	8	8	8
C				3	3	3	3	3
D					8	8	8	8
E						8	8	8
F							8	8
G								8
H								

Table 6.18. Correlation Matrix for Constructs

Construct	1	2	3	4	5	6	7	8
1		7	7	7	8	8	8	8
2			8	8	7	7	7	7
3				8	7	7	7	7
4					7	7	7	7
5						8	8	8
6							8	8
7								8
8								

Table 6.19. Correlation Matrix for Constructs

Construct	1	2	3	4	5	6	7	8
1		3	3	3	4	4	4	4
2			4	4	3	3	3	3
3				4	3	3	3	3
4					3	3	3	3
5						4	4	4
6							4	4
7								4
8								

Changes in the Intelligibility of Descriptions of Effective Teaching and Learning

For John, these changes were shown by the changes in the coefficients of consistency and plausibility which occurred throughout the program. They are summarized as follows:

Grid number	1	2	Adjusted 2	3	Adjusted 3
Coefficient of consistency	0.83	0.59	0.83	0.84	1.0
Coefficient of plausibility	0.57	0.24	0.75	0.86	1.0

As previously discussed, the decrease in both consistency and plausibility from grid 1 to grid 2, that is between weeks 1 and 2 of the program, may indicate that, although John was aware of an increase in possible ways of describing effective teaching and learning, he was unable to accommodate these into a coherent set of elements. The coefficients for adjusted grid 2 support this suggestion, and indicate John's retention of a core set of factors in describing effective teaching and learning.

The wider range of referents used in the elements of grid 3 completed at the end of the program and, in particular, the higher coefficient of plausibility indicate that John has been able to accommodate an increased range of educational perspectives in his description of effective teaching and learning. The high correlation of the constructs for grid 3, as indicated by the high coefficient of plausibility, shows that, for John, the description given by the elements can be plausibly interpreted in terms of the constructs. This description is highly consistent and plausible, and hence intelligible. The one factor not intelligibly accommodated by John appears to be the notion of a core curriculum.

The changes in these coefficients throughout the program indicate that the intelligibility of the description of effective teaching and learning given by John has increased during the program, not in terms of its consistency, but in terms of its plausibility. This appears to indicate that, in providing John with a wide range of eductional perspectives through studying various approaches to curriculum development, the program has not helped John to change the logical consistency of his descriptions, but has increased his capacity to give plausible interpretations of these descriptions. That is, a core of factors for describing effective teaching and learning has been retained by John, but these factors may now be given more plausible interpretations. John is better at giving more practically plausible interpretations of the conditions for effective teaching and learning for his focus class.

Case Study B (Further Education)

Mary is a senior nurse educator responsible for a post-certificate course in midwifery at a large public hospital. She has extensive experience as a nurse educator, and has completed some studies towards the degree of Master of Educational Studies. She has considerable autonomy in the presentation of this course, but the approach taken to student assessment for the course is restricted by requirements from external examining bodies.

The focus class was of fifteen (one male and fourteen female) certificated nurses, each with a minimum of one and a half years of post-graduation experience. A small number of nurses had more than twenty years' such experience. The age range was 22–50 years. The course being taken for six hours per week was midwifery, as a post-certificate course. The nurses undertaking the course were selected from a large number of applicants and were, therefore, highly motivated. They came from a range of widely differing previous hospital experiences.

Repertory Grid 1

Elements of the Grid

Mary completed an initial set of statements of the conditions for effective teaching and learning for her focus class. These elements were as follows:

Element	Effective teaching and learning occurs when
A	The curriculum is based on knowledge and skills brought by the students as entering behaviour.
B	Learning experiences are based on previous experiences.
C	The strategies employed utilize a student's preferred style of learning.
D	The students assist in the planning of their learning experiences.
E	Self-evaluation is used as the basis for different learning needs.

F   Group cooperation is encouraged.
G   The student is actively involved in the learning process.
H   A wide perspective of the subject is presented.
I   The teacher is competent in the area being taught.

Constructs (Bipolar Statements)

Using the triad method, Mary elicited the following bipolar constructs from the set of elements given above:

Construct	Initial pole	Emergent pole
1	Learning is based on individual needs.	Learning is most effective when the students' style of learning is matched.
2	Learning grows from previous experience.	Learning increases with student involvement in planning.
3	Effective learning depends on student involvement in planning.	Learning occurs when students negotiate learning strategies.
4	Learning occurs when students define their own learning needs.	Group cooperation increases learning.
5	Active participation is necessary for effective learning.	Self-assessment increases learning.
6	Motivation is increased if application to work/life experiences is increased.	Group cooperation encourages learning.
7	Learning is increased if not limited by syllabus boundaries.	Students learn more easily if the teacher is perceived as competent in the clinical field.
8	Learning occurs if the information provided acknowledges the students' starting points.	Students learn more easily if the teacher is perceived as competent in the theoretical field.
9	Learning occurs when the teacher is at ease with the chosen strategies.	Learning occurs when it is individualized.

Table 6.20. Repertory Grid 1

Construct	Elements									Construct
Initial pole	A	B	C	D	E	F	G	H	I	Emergent pole
C1P1	✓	✓	X	✓	✓	X	✓	X	X	C1P2
C2P1	✓	✓	X	X	X	✓	X	✓	X	C2P2
C3P1	✓	X	✓	✓	✓	✓	✓	X	X	C3P2
C4P1	X	✓	✓	✓	✓	X	✓	X	✓	C4P2
C5P1	✓	X	X	X	X	✓	✓	✓	✓	C5P2
C6P1	✓	✓	X	✓	✓	X	✓	✓	✓	C6P2
C7P1	X	X	X	✓	✓	✓	X	✓	X	C7P2
C8P1	✓	✓	✓	✓	✓	✓	✓	X	X	C8P2
C9P1	X	✓	✓	✓	X	✓	X	✓	✓	C9P2

Completion of the Repertory Grid

Using the procedures described in Chapter 2, Mary then completed the repertory grid as shown in Table 6.20.

Correlation Matrices for Elements and Constructs

The correlation matrices for both the elements and the constructs were completed by Mary and are shown as Tables 6.21 and 6.22. The adjusted construct correlation matrix is shown in Table 6.23.

Calculation of Coefficients of Consistency and Plausibility

These were calculated as 0.48 and 0.27 respectively.

Correlation of the elements. Mary then considered the correlation of the elements of her first grid, first, in terms of their co-referencing, which is shown in Table 6.24. This analysis indicates very little co-referencing. Students are referred to as follows:

Table 6.21.   Correlation Matrix for Elements

Element	A	B	C	D	E	F	G	H	I
A		4	3	4	5	5	7	4	3
B			4	5	6	2	6	3	4
C				6	5	5	5	2	5
D					8	4	6	3	4
E						3	6	2	3
F							3	6	3
G								2	2
H									6
I									

Table 6.22.   Correlation Matrix for Constructs

Construct	1	2	3	4	5	6	7	8	9
1		5	6	6	3	7	4	7	12
2			3	1	6	4	5	4	4
3				5	4	4	5	8	4
4					2	6	3	6	4
5						5	4	3	5
6							4	5	3
7								3	6
8									3
9									

Table 6.23. Correlation Matrix for Constructs

Construct	1	2	3	4	5	6	7	8	9
1		0	1	1	2	2	1	2	4
2			2	4	1	1	0	1	1
3				0	1	1	0	3	1
4					3	1	2	1	1
5						0	1	2	0
6							1	0	2
7								2	1
8									2
9									

Table 6.24. Referents for Elements

Element	Referents			
	R1	R2	R3	R4
A	Curriculum	Knowledge and skills	Students	Entering behaviour
B	Learning experiences	Previous experiences		
C	Strategies (teaching)	Student	Preferred style of learning	
D	Students	Planning	Learning experiences	
E	Self-evaluation	Learning needs		
F	Group cooperation			
G	Student	Learning process		
H	Subject	Wide perspective		
I	Teacher	Area (being taught)		

Element A (Referent 3)
C (R2),
D (R1),
E (R1), and
G (R1)

This suggests a higher correlation between elements A, C, D, E and G due to co-referencing. That is, for Mary, these elements may be explicitly related through their reference to students.

If a grid consisting of elements A, C, D, E and G only is examined, the coefficient of consistency is found to be 0.61. Similarly, the co-efficients of consistency for grids consisting of the elements listed are:

Elements	Coefficients of consistency
A–I	0.48
A, B, C, D, E, G	0.60
A, C, D, E, G	0.61
D, E, G	0.66

An inspection of the grid indicates that the maximum coefficient of consistency will be obtained using the set of elements D, E and G. These elements are:

D   The students assist in the planning of their learning experiences.
E   Self-evaluation is used as the basis for different learning needs.
G   The student is actively involved in the learning process.

The emphasis on these three elements was acknowledged by Mary, who commented:

> On analysis, the area of commonality is that the curriculum is based on an active student participation. This requires the students to assist in the planning of the curriculum, based on the individual and group needs, and the starting point is the student/group previous experiences. Self-evaluation is necessary to define these learning needs. The underlying assumption is that the curriculum is strongly student-centred.

A further inspection of the grid shows that elements D, E and G are perfectly correlated with the initial poles of constructs 1, 2, 3, 4, 6 and 8. Thus elements D, E and G have been interpreted to mean:

C1P1 Learning is based on individual needs.

C2P1 Learning grows from previous experience.

C3P1 Effective learning depends on student involvement in planning.

C4P1 Learning occurs when students define their own learning needs.

C6P1 Motivation is increased if application to work/life experiences is obvious.

C8P1 Learning occurs if the information provided acknowledges the students' starting points.

Thus when elements D, E and G are interpreted to mean the above statements, the description provided by elements D, E and G is perfectly consistent and plausible. This is, for Mary, the core grid from which much of her interpretation of effective teaching and learning will arise. The completed core grid is shown as Table 6.25.

This grid has coefficients of consistency and plausibility of 1.0. The description provided by elements D, E and G is highly intelligible, but the addition of other elements lowers the intelligibility considerably. As for John, it may be concluded that Mary has a core description which is highly intelligible. However, attempts to incorporate additional factors into the description result in a loss in intelligibility, particularly in the consistency of the elements.

Repertory Grid 2

Elements of the Grid

At the end of the second week Mary completed her second repertory grid. The elements were as follows:

Element	Effective learning and teaching occurs when
A	The starting point for the lesson is based on the students' previous experience.
B	The sequencing of the subject-matter is negotiated with the students, based on their perceived needs.
C	Learning is encouraged through experience.
D	Individual values, both of the teacher and the learner, are considered within the learning process.
E	The need to encourage understanding of knowledge is emphasized.

Table 6.25.   Core Repertory Grid

Construct	Element			Construct
Initial statement	D	E	G	Emergent statement
C1P1	✓	✓	✓	C1P2
C2P1	✓	✓	✓	C2P2
C3P1	✓	✓	✓	C3P2
C4P1	✓	✓	✓	C4P2
C6P1	✓	✓	✓	C6P2
C8P1	✓	✓	✓	C8P2

F   The teaching strategies used equate with the purposes of the lesson and type of knowledge.

G   Self-assessment of learning needs and development is encouraged.

H   Students are encouraged to share their individual learning experiences.

I   Social expectations are discussed as a basis for developing understanding.

Constructs of the Grid

Using the triad method, Mary elicited from the set of elements the following set of bipolar constructs:

Construct	Initial pole	Emergent pole
1	Experience forms the basis of learning.	Sequencing within the curriculum is negotiable.
2	Knowledge is subjective.	Values cannot be separated from learning.
3	Understanding is of prime importance.	Values are personal.
4	Teaching strategies relate to the type of knowledge.	Values are personal.
5	Individual learning needs form the basis of curriculum development.	Teaching styles relate to the purposes of the curriculum.

6	Teaching strategies should encourage student participation.	Assessment should be based on individual development.
7	Learning is individual.	The curriculum should consider social expectations.
8	Student participation is essential.	Community attitudes should be considered in the learning process.
9	Learning should be based on experience.	Community attitudes should be considered in the learning process.

Completion of the Repertory Grid

Mary then completed the repertory grid as shown in Table 6.26.

Correlation Matrices for Elements and Constructs

The correlation matrices for both the elements and the constructs were completed by Mary and are shown in Tables 6.27 and 6.28.

Calculation of Coefficients of Consistency and Plausibility

These were calculated as 0.50 and 0.29 respectively.

The median construct correlation score is 5. Hence the adjusted construct correlation matrix is as shown in Table 6.29.

Interpretation of the Repertory Grids, Correlation Matrices and Coefficients of Consistency and Plausibility

Mary's examination of the referents of the elements showed that there was very limited co-referencing.

An examination of the correlation matrix for the elements showed that the following pairs of elements were highly correlated.

Table 6.26.   Repertory Grid 2

Construct	Elements									Construct
Initial pole	A	B	C	D	E	F	G	H	I	Emergent pole
C1P1	✓	X	✓	X	X	✓	X	✓	✓	C1P2
C2P1	✓	X	✓	X	✓	✓	X	✓	X	C2P2
C3P1	✓	X	✓	X	✓	X	X	✓	X	C3P2
C4P1	X	X	X	X	✓	✓	X	X	X	C4P2
C5P1	✓	✓	X	✓	✓	X	✓	✓	X	C5P2
C6P1	✓	X	✓	X	✓	✓	X	✓	✓	C6P2
C7P1	✓	✓	✓	✓	✓	X	✓	✓	X	C7P2
C8P1	✓	✓	✓	X	X	X	✓	✓	X	C8P2
C9P1	✓	✓	✓	X	X	X	✓	✓	X	C9P2

Table 6.27.   Correlation Matrix for Elements

Element	A	B	C	D	E	F	G	H	I
A		5	8	3	5	3	4	9	3
B			4	7	3	1	9	5	3
C				2	4	4	4	8	4
D					5	3	7	3	5
E						5	3	5	3
F							1	3	7
G								5	3
H									3
I									

Table 6.28. Correlation Matrix for Constructs

Construct	1	2	3	4	5	6	7	8	9
1		7	6	4	2	8	3	5	5
2			8	6	4	8	5	5	5
3				5	5	7	6	6	6
4					3	5	2	2	2
5						3	8	5	6
6							4	4	4
7								7	7
8									9
9									

Table 6.29. Adjusted Correlation Matrix for Constructs

Construct	1	2	3	4	5	6	7	8	9
1		2	1	1	3	3	2	0	0
2			3	1	1	3	0	0	0
3				0	0	2	1	1	1
4					2	0	3	3	3
5						2	3	0	1
6							1	1	1
7								2	2
8									4
9									

Pair of elements	Correlation score
A, H	9
A, C	8
C, H	8
B, D	7
D, G	7
I, F	7

This suggested to Mary that:

i element E does not correlate highly with any other elements, and can be removed from the grid;

ii elements I and F correlate highly with one another, but not with any other elements; on this basis they may be removed from the grid, and their relationship treated separately;

iii the remaining elements may be treated as two groups of elements, namely, group of elements A, C and H, and group of elements B, D and G.

The coefficients of consistency for the grids formed from the above combinations of elements are:

Grid elements	Coefficient of consistency
Complete grid	0.50
Grid less element E	0.51
Elements E, I and F	0.55
Grid less elements I and F	0.55
Grid less elements E, I and F	0.78
Elements B, D and G	0.85
Elements A, C and H	0.93

Hence, for Mary,

i there is little increase in consistency by eliminating element E;

ii there is only a marginal increase in consistency by eliminating elements I and F;

iii there is a substantial increase in consistency by eliminating elements E, I and F, even though this set of elements is not highly consistent;

iv the grids formed from elements B, D and G, and A, C and H are highly consistent.

Table 6.30. Adjusted Repertory Grid

Construct	Elements						Construct
Initial pole	A	B	C	D	G	H	Emergent pole
C4P2	✓	✓	✓	✓	✓	✓	C4P1
C5P1	✓	✓	X	✓	✓	✓	C5P2
C7P1	✓	✓	✓	✓	✓	✓	C7P2
C8P1	✓	✓	✓	X	✓	✓	C8P2
CP1	✓	✓	✓	X	✓	✓	C9P2

An inspection of the grid indicates that, if the poles of construct C4 are reversed, the higher correlations will result. An inspection also reveals that constructs C1, C2, C3 and C6 do not strongly discriminate between the elements. If elements E, F and I are eliminated from the grid, the poles of construct 4 are reversed, and the non–discriminating constructs C1, C2, C3 and C6 removed, then the grid becomes as shown in Table 6.30.

An inspection of this grid shows that a grid consisting of elements A, B, G and H shows perfect correlation of both elements and the initial poles of the constructs C5, C7, C8 and C9, and the emergent pole of C4. Thus the description of effective teaching and learning given by elements A, B, G and H is the most consistent and plausible description available for Mary's focus class from the original set of elements. This description is:

A   The starting point for the lesson is based on the students' previous experiences.

B   The sequencing of the subject–matter is negotiated with the students, based on their perceived needs.

G   Self-assessment of learning needs and development is encouraged.

H   Students are encouraged to share their individual learning experiences.

For Mary, these statements give the most consistent and plausible, and hence intelligible, description of effective teaching and learning for her focus class.

For Repertory Grid 1, the core elements were found to be elements D, E and G. These were:

D   The students assist in the planning of their learning experiences.
E   Self-evaluation is used as the basis for different learning needs.
G   The student is actively involved in the learning process.

A comparison of the elements in these two sets of core elements, for weeks 1 and 2 of the program, indicates that: element E (Repertory Grid 1) is very similar to element G (Repertory Grid 2); element D (Repertory Grid 1) — 'The students assist in the planning of their learning experiences' — has been elaborated in Repertory Grid 2 to include element A — 'The starting point for the lesson is based on the students' previous experiences' and element B — 'The sequencing of the subject is negotiated with the students, based on their perceived needs.' Element H of Repertory Grid 2 refers to shared learning experiences, and this, in part, may be what is meant by element G (Repertory Grid 1) — 'The student is actively involved in the learning process.' Hence the core elements of Repertory Grid 2 are an elaboration of the core elements of Repertory Grid 1, with the ideas of student-teacher negotiation and the sharing of learning experiences between students being introduced into the description by Mary.

Repertory Grid 3

Elements of the Grid

The following elements were given for this repertory grid completed at the end of the teacher development program.

Element   Effective teaching and learning occurs when
A   Active student participation is encouraged.
B   The curriculum is negotiated within the constraints of the Nurses Registration Board Guidelines.
C   Self-assessment is encouraged.
D   Individual perspectives form the basis for discussion and learning.
E   Teaching strategies are student-centred.
F   Relationships between theory and practice are emphasized.
G   Language is appropriate to the content of the learning.

Constructs (Bipolar Statements)

Using the triad method, Mary elicited the following pairs of bipolar constructs:

Construct	Initial pole	Emergent pole
1	Active student participation is essential.	There is a core curriculum.
2	Some aspects of the curriculum are negotiable.	Individual perspectives are important within the curriculum.
3	Entry behaviour forms the basis for curriculum planning.	A wide range of teaching strategies should be used.
4	Learning must be seen to be relevant.	Individual differences are discussed.
5	All learning should be initially evaluated.	Experience is the basis for curriculum planning.
6	Learning strategies should be practical.	Negotiation skills should be taught.
7	Assessment is formal.	Individual values must be considered.

Completing the Repertory Grid

The repertory grid was then completed as shown in Table 6.31.

Correlation Matrices for Elements and Constructs

The correlation matrices for both the elements and constructs were computed, and are shown in Tables 6.32 and 6.33 respectively.

Calculation of Coefficients of Consistency and Plausibility

These were then calculated as 0.44 and 0.24 respectively.

The medians of the construct correlation scores are 3 and 4. The adjusted correlation matrix is as shown in Table 6.34.

Table 6.31. Repertory Grid

Construct	Elements							Construct
Initial pole	A	B	C	D	E	F	G	Emergent pole
C1P1	√	X	√	√	√	X	X	C1P2
C2P1	√	√	X	X	X	√	√	C2P2
C3P1	√	√	√	√	X	X	X	C3P2
C4P1	X	√	X	√	√	√	X	C4P2
C5P1	X	√	√	X	X	√	√	C5P2
C6P1	X	√	X	√	√	√	X	C6P2
C7P1	√	X	X	X	X	√	X	C7P2

Table 6.32. Correlation Matrix for Elements

Elements	A	B	C	D	E	F	G
A		3	4	3	2	2	3
B			2	3	2	6	3
C				4	3	1	4
D					6	2	1
E						3	2
F							4
G							

Table 6.33. Correlation Matrix for Constructs

Construct	1	2	3	4	5	6	7
1		1	5	3	1	3	2
2			3	3	5	3	6
3				3	3	3	4
4					3	7	3
5						3	4
6							4
7							

Table 6.34.   *Adjusted Correlation Matrix for Constructs*

Construct	C1	C2	C3	C4	C5	C6	C7
C1		2	1	0	2	0	1
C2			0	0	1	0	2
C3				0	0	0	1
C4					0	3	0
C5						0	1
C6							1
C7							

Interpretation of the Repertory Grids, Correlation Matrices and Coefficients of Consistency and Plausibility

In examining these grids and their correlation matrices, Mary concluded that there was very limited co-referencing between the elements of the grid. An inspection of the repertory grid showed that the following pairs of elements were highly correlated.

Pairs of elements	Correlation score
B and F	6/7
E and D	6/7

If, on this basis, elements A, C and G are eliminated, the grid becomes as shown in Table 6.35.

A further inspection indicates that only constructs C4 and C6 are highly discriminatory. Hence the grid may be reduced to the following:

Construct	Elements	Construct
Initial pole	B D E F	Emergent pole
C4P1		C4P2
C6P1		C6P2

In this case the coefficients of consistency and plausibility are both 1.0. Thus the elements B, D, E and F give the most consistent and plausible description of effective teaching and learning for Mary for her focus class. This description is as follows:

Table 6.35. Adjusted Repertory Grid

Construct	Elements				Construct
Initial pole	B	D	E	F	Emergent pole
C1P1	X	✓	✓	X	C1P2
C2P1	✓	X	X	✓	C2P2
C3P1	✓	✓	X	X	C3P2
C4P1	✓	✓	✓	✓	C4P2
C5P1	✓	X	X	✓	C5P2
C6P1	✓	✓	✓	✓	C6P2
C7P1	✓	X	X	✓	C7P2

B   The curriculum is negotiated within the constraints of the Nurses Registration Board guidelines.

D   Individual perspectives form the basis for discussion and learning.

E   Teaching strategies are student-centred.

F   Relationships between theory and practice are emphasized.

Comparison of Interpretations of Repertory Grids 1, 2 and 3

In making this comparison, Mary commented:

> The language used in Repertory Grid 3 was more active, and demonstrated a closer ability to look at my own teaching. Possibly, the terms used, and the concepts outlined, were more closely aligned to the reality of my teaching in opposition to the ideal.

> Some areas were omitted from Grid 3. For example, no mention was made of environment or of teacher competencies. I feel the former has probably lost significance if emphasis is on the individual. . . .

> I feel many elements in Grid 1 were sublimated into one related to negotiation in Grid 3, for example, group cohesiveness. Also the overall concept portrayed in Grid 3 was one of adult learning, negating the need to include this as an actual element.

Table 6.36. *Consistency and Plausibility for the Three Grids*

Grid number	1	2	3
Coefficient of consistency	0.48	0.50	0.44
Coefficient of plausibility	0.27	0.29	0.24

As supported by Mary's comments, each of the sets of elements produced for the three repertory grids contained a core set of elements. As the program progressed, this core became more closely focused on Mary's role as a teacher and, in particular, on practical constraints, such as the Nurses Registration Board. Whilst Mary wished to teach in a style involving a high level of student interaction and negotiation, constraints, including the requirement to relate 'theory to practice', were perceived to impinge heavily on that style.

In addition, the emphasis on the learner as an individual and on adult learning was seen to remove the need to mention factors such as the learning environment and teacher competence. These factors have been 'sublimated into one related to negotiation'; that is, the notion of negotiation is being used by Mary to attempt to achieve a highly consistent and plausible description of effective teaching and learning. The teacher's success in teaching effectively, as this role is now perceived, will be dependent upon translating this notion into the practice and skills of teaching. The coefficients of consistency and plausibility for the three grids developed throughout the program are as shown in Table 6.36. There is no marked change in either the consistency or plausibility of the descriptions of effective teaching and learning given throughout the program.

The lack of success by Mary in giving a more consistent and plausible description of effective teaching and learning, and hence a more intelligible description, and the continuing conflict between her preferred teaching style and practical constraints on this teaching are illustrated by the low levels of the coefficients of consistency and plausibility throughout the program.

Case Study C (Primary Education)

Andrew is a vice-principal in a large primary school (grades K-6) with particular responsibility for the learning program of grades 3 to 6. He has a first degree and a Diploma of Education, and is, therefore, a four-year trained teacher. Prior to accepting his present position, he was the principal of a small country primary school. The teacher development program was undertaken as part of his studies towards the degree of Master of Educational Studies.

The class selected was a group of eight grade 5/6 students. This group is withdrawn from their normal class for a set period each day of the teaching week, and for a total time of two hours for that week. All members of the group had poorly developed language skills. All of the group were boys with very low levels of self-esteem.

Repertory Grid 1

Elements of the Grid

Andrew's initial description of the conditions for effective teaching and learning for his focus group included the following elements.

Element
A	Children learn most effectively when their individual needs are recognized.
B	Effective learning involves self-motivation.
C	Effective learning involves interaction between the teacher and the learner.
D	Children need to feel a sense of individual worth.
E	Effective learning involves practical experiences.
F	The learner should have a sense of purpose and direction.
G	The learning program should consider the whole child.
H	Children learn at different rates.
I	Active participation by the learner is necessary for effective learning.
J	Learners should evaluate their own learning needs.

Constructs of the Grid

Using the triad method, the following constructs were elicited.

Construct	Initial pole	Emergent pole
1	Effective learning involves interaction between the learners.	Effective learning involves the learner's own initiatives.

2	Effective learning depends on individual learners' attitudes.	Effective learning depends on the attitudes that develop from the relationship between teacher and learner.
3	Effective learning is learner-centred.	Effective learning requires teacher input.
4	Effective learning focuses on individual needs.	Effective learning focuses on the needs of the curriculum.
5	Effective learning is based on practical experiences.	Effective learning precedes practical experiences.
6	Effective learning needs to be purposeful for the learner.	Effective learning needs to be purposeful for the teacher.
7	Children learn at different rates.	Children learn at the same rate.
8	Effective learning involves self-evaluation by the learner.	Effective learning involves external evaluation of the learner.
9	Effective learning focuses on the whole child.	Effective learning focuses on specific developmental areas of the child.
10	The learner should be actively involved in the learning process.	The learner should learn from a teacher model.

Repertory Grid

The repertory grid is shown in Table 6.37.

Correlation Matrices

The correlation matrices are shown as Tables 6.38 and 6.39.

Coefficients of Consistency and Plausibility

These were found to be 0.77 and 0.49 respectively.
   The adjusted construct correlation matrix is as shown in Table 6.40.

Table 6.37. Repertory Grid 1

Construct	Elements										Construct
Initial pole	A	B	C	D	E	F	G	H	I	J	Emergent pole
C1P1	√	X	√	√	√	X	√	√	X	X	C1P2
C2P1	X	√	X	X	√	√	X	X	√	√	C2P2
C3P1	X	√	X	X	√	√	X	√	√	√	C3P2
C4P1	√	√	√	√	√	√	√	√	√	√	C4P2
C5P1	√	√	√	√	√	√	√	√	√	√	C5P2
C6P1	√	√	√	√	√	√	√	√	√	√	C6P2
C7P1	√	√	√	√	√	√	√	√	√	√	C7P2
C8P1	X	√	X	√	√	√	X	X	√	√	C8P2
C9P1	√	√	√	√	√	√	√	√	√	√	C9P2
C10P1	√	√	√	√	√	√	√	√	√	√	C10P2

Table 6.38. Correlation Matrix for Elements

Element	A	B	C	D	E	F	G	H	I	J
A		6	10	9	7	6	7	8	6	6
B			6	7	9	10	6	7	10	10
C				9	7	6	10	9	6	6
D					8	7	9	8	7	7
E						9	7	8	9	9
F							6	7	10	10
G								9	6	6
H									7	7
I										10
J										

Table 6.39.   Correlation Matrix for Constructs

Construct	1	2	3	4	5	6	7	8	9	10
1		1	2	6	6	6	6	2	6	6
2			9	5	5	5	5	9	5	5
3				6	6	6	6	8	6	6
4					10	10	10	6	10	10
5						10	10	6	10	10
6							10	6	10	10
7								6	10	10
8									6	6
9										10
10										

Table 6.40.   Adjusted Correlation Matrix for Constructs

Construct	1	2	3	4	5	6	7	8	9	10
1		4	3	1	1	1	1	3	1	1
2			3	0	0	0	0	3	0	0
3				1	1	1	1	2	1	1
4					5	5	5	1	5	5
5						5	5	1	5	5
6							5	1	5	5
7								1	5	5
8									1	1
9										5
10										

Interpretation of Correlation Matrices and Coefficients

Correlation of elements. In interpreting the grid and its correlation matrices, Andrew focused on those pairs of elements with low correlations of 6/10. Comments made on the various groups of elements were as follows:

> Elements A and B: The teacher's perceived needs of the individual may not be seen by the individual as being in their own interests.

> Elements B and C: The teacher-learner interaction does not always help to motivate the child. Does this mean that the children would prefer a more structured, teacher-directed situation? This applies to my focus class, where the self-esteem of the children is very low, and, in order to motivate the group, strong teacher input is necessary.

> Elements A and F: This confirms the above, since recognition of needs did not correlate highly with the learner's sense of purpose. It also indicates a need to focus on self-esteem itself as an area of learning.

> Elements B and G: If we are focusing on the whole child, we are focusing on his strengths and weaknesses. If we are asking the children to focus on weaknesses, then it becomes a delicate issue for them to accept the weakness, and to become motivated to resolving it.

> Elements G, I and J: The interaction places as much emphasis on the role of the teacher as it does on the role of the learner. I have a philosophy of the teacher as a facilitator of learning. With my focus class, I provide more direction than I may in a different class. This is true of my teaching style in this school, when compared with the schools in which I have previously taught. This is supported by the low correlation between G, I and J.

However, when Andrew contrasted these comments with his interpretation of the high correlations obtained, he concluded that:

> My argument to date is countered by these correlations. Perhaps this highlights a conflict between my teaching philosophy and my teaching style at my current school. It also indicates the fundamental importance of teacher-pupil relationships, and the difficulties the

teacher has in meeting the needs of the individual as perceived by the individual, and as perceived by the teacher.

These comments highlight the extent to which interpreting the correlation matrix of the elements of a repertory grid on effective teaching and learning can involve the teacher in a consideration of fundamental professional issues.

Correlation of constructs. Andrew's comments on those pairs of constructs with low correlations were as follows:

Constructs 1 and 2 (1/10)
The low correlation can be explained by the way the poles were recorded. If the poles of construct 2 were reversed, then these would be a high correlation. Constructs 1 and 2 are similar, and could have been combined.

Constructs 1 and 3 (2/10)
The low correlation reinforces the statements relating to teacher-learner input.

Constructs 1 and 8 (2/10)
The low correlation does not fit with my focus class, where personal and immediate feedback is important. However, if we look at the two poles that do correlate we see that there is a high correlation between learner initiations and self-evaluation.

In discussing those constructs with high correlations, he commented as follows:

Constructs 4, 5, 6, 7, 9 and 10 (Their initial poles) are integral parts of the educational philosophy as outlined in the Committee on Primary Education (COPE) report (1972) for primary education in Tasmania.

For primary teachers, these are fundamental to the learning process. As a result, this only confirms my view of teaching. More value may have been gained by making the constructs less bipolar. This is necessary to enable a more critical look at the widely accepted beliefs outlined above.

Focusing the grid. If, in the light of the above comments, constructs C1, C2, C3 and C8 are removed, the resulting grid of elements A to J and constructs C4, C5, C6, C7, C9 and C10 is perfectly correlated. In this case the coefficients of consistency and plausibility are both 1. However, as previously commented by Andrew, the description of effective teaching and learning, and the interpretation of this provided by the initial poles of the above constructs, does not go beyond that provided by the COPE report (1972). Constructs whose poles discriminate between the educational issues involved are required.

Andrew began the program with a highly consistent and plausible description of effective teaching and learning, but with some personal doubts about the matching of his educational philosophy and the teaching style adopted for the focus class.

Repertory Grid 2

At the end of the second week Andrew completed a second grid using the following elements.

Element	Statement of element
A	Efficient teaching provides significant experiences that enable the children to change their attitude to learning.
B	Efficient learning involves a balance between what the child receives and what he gives.
C	Efficient learning involves tasks that should be personally relevant to the learner.
D	Efficient teaching and learning involves interaction between the teacher and learner.
E	The teacher should provide a discovery model of learning.
F	Efficient learning involves learner awareness of his own rate of development.
G	Efficient teaching and learning is based on an awareness of language as central to the learning process.
H	Efficient teaching involves an awareness of appropriate teaching and learning methods and styles.
I	Efficient learning involves learner awareness of the overall context of the learning.
J	Efficient teaching involves teacher awareness of individual learning rates.

Constructs

Construct	Initial pole	Emergent pole
C1	Learning is based on personally relevant experiences.	Learning is a balance between personal experiences and given experiences.
C2	Interaction between teacher and learner occurs through the the teacher approaching learning from the student's standpoint.	Interaction between teacher and learner occurs by the teacher becoming a learner with the learner.
C3	An awareness of rates of development occurs through a discovery.	An awareness of rates of development occurs through language.
C4	Appropriate methods and styles are based on individual rates.	Appropriate methods and styles are based on the language used.
C5	The teacher's methods and styles provide an awareness of the overall context of teaching.	Language provides an awareness of the overall context of teaching.
C6	Interaction between the teachers and the learners should be language-based.	Interaction between the teachers and the learners should be experience-based.
C7	A balanced learning approach is achieved by an awareness of the overall learning context.	A balanced learning approach is provided by the learner's self-awareness of his development.
C8	Significant learning experiences can be provided by a variety of teaching approaches.	Significant learning experiences can be provided by a teacher adopting a discovery model of learning.
C9	Relevance for the learner arises from the language used.	Relevance for the learner arises from matching the tasks to the individual learning rates.

Table 6.41.   Repertory Grid 2

Construct	Elements										Construct
Initial pole	A	B	C	D	E	F	G	H	I	J	Emergent pole
C1P1	√	X	√	X	X	√	X	X	X	X	C1P2
C2P1	√	X	√	√	X	X	√	√	√	√	C2P2
C3P1	√	X	√	X	√	√	X	√	√	√	C3P2
C4P1	√	X	√	X	√	√	X	√	√	√	C4P2
C5P1	√	√	√	X	√	√	X	√	√	√	C5P2
C6P1	X	X	X	X	X	X	√	√	√	√	C6P2
C7P1	X	√	√	√	√	X	√	√	√	√	C7P2
C8P1	√	√	√	√	X	X	√	√	√	√	C8P2
C9P1	X	X	X	X	X	X	√	X	X	X	C9P2
C10P1	X	X	X	X	X	√	X	X	X	X	C10P2

C10	Interaction between the teacher and learner occurs with a discovery model of learning.	Interaction between the teacher and learner occurs through the individual's assessment of his needs.

Repertory Grid

The repertory grid was completed as shown in Table 6.41.

As the teacher was unable to complete the grid for elements H, I and J, these have been excluded from the grid when completing the correlation matrices.

Correlaton Matrices and Coefficients

Correlation of elements. The correlation matrix for elements is given in Table 6.42.

Correlation of constructs. The correlation matrix for the constructs is given in Table 6.43.

Table 6.42. *Correlation Matrix for Elements*

Element	A	B	C	D	E	F	G
A		5	10	5	5	9	3
B			5	8	6	6	6
C				5	5	7	3
D					4	4	8
E						6	2
F							2
G							

Table 6.43. *Correlation Matrix for Constructs*

Construct	C1	C2	C3	C4	C5	C6	C7	C8	C9	C10
C1		4	6	6	5	3	0	3	3	3
C2			3	3	2	4	3	6	4	2
C3				7	6	2	1	2	2	4
C4					6	2	1	2	2	4
C5						1	2	3	1	3
C6							4	3	7	5
C7								4	4	4
C8									3	1
C9										5
C10										

The median construct correlation scores are 3 and 4. The adjusted construct correlation matrix is shown in Table 6.44.

Interpretation of Correlation Matrices and Coefficients of Consistency and Plausibility

Correlation of elements. In considering those groups of elements with a high correlation, Andrew made the following comments:

Table 6.44. *Adjusted Correlation Matrix for Constructs*

Construct	C1	C2	C3	C4	C5	C6	C7	C8	C9	C10
C1		0	2	2	1	1	3	0	0	0
C2			0	0	1	0	0	2	0	1
C3				3	2	1	2	1	1	0
C4					2	1	2	1	1	0
C5						2	1	0	2	0
C6							0	0	3	1
C7								0	0	0
C8									0	2
C9										1
C10										

Elements A and C
These two elements could be combined, successfully, to read:

'Efficient teaching provides personally relevant and significant experiences that enable the learner to develop positive attitudes towards learning.'

Elements A and F
I have had difficulty in justifying element F (Efficient learning involves learner awareness of his own rate of development). The high correlation between A and F classifies my thoughts in this way. The learner's awareness of his rates of development does not necessarily involve knowledge of learning theories. It involves a sense of progress, a sense of achievement, a sense of competence. Thus, the significant experiences in this context are those experiences which provide the learner with a sense of development. Element F is rewritten as: 'Efficient learning involves a learner sense of development.'

Elements B and D
These two elements could be successfully combined to read:
'Efficient teaching and learning involves a balanced interaction between the teacher and the learner.'

Elements C and F
Given my description of awareness of rates of development above, the relevance of the learning tasks and the learner's sense of development are closely related. The issue is whether relevance leads to a sense of development, or whether a sense of development provides relevance to the learning, Both directions are legitimate, and should be recognized. Perhaps, I should go a step further, and state that a task is relevant if it provides a sense of development.

Elements E and F
An awareness of development is an integral part of the discovery model of learning.

Elements H, I and J
Appropriate teaching and learning styles are those which provide an awareness of the learning context and which take into account individuals. Elements H and I could be combined to read:

'Efficient teaching involves an awareness of individual teaching and learning styles.'

For the reasons given above, the teacher revised the elements of the grid. These elements, and the comments made by the teacher, are as follows:

Revised Elements
A. Efficient teaching provides personally relevant and significant experiences that enable the learner to develop positive attitudes towards learning.

This raises the issue as to which experiences are relevant and how this is decided. It presumes emphasis on individual needs. It requires the teacher to make continual judgments about the curricula, balancing social needs with individual needs.

B. Efficient teaching and learning involves a balanced interaction between the teacher and the learner.

This presumes a learning relationship based on mutual respect. It involves a balance between teacher-directed learning and learner-initiated learning.

C. Efficient teaching involves an awareness of individual teaching and learning styles.

One way of describing different teaching styles is as follows:

teaching from a teacher's viewpoint, i.e. the master to the student;

teaching from the learner's viewpoint, e.g. teaching according to states of development;

learning with the learner, i.e. the teacher is very much a facilitator in the learning process.

Effective teaching depends on the judgments made within this continuum; when to facilitate, when to respond to needs, when to tell!

D. Efficient learning involves a learner sense of development.

This relates closely to Element A. The learner needs to want to learn and to see himself as learning. This involves self-esteem, personal goals, teacher feedback, self-motivation, etc.

E. Efficient teaching and learning involves an awareness of language as central to the learning process.

A key issue is how much learning is an internal process and how much learning depends on relationships with others and the communication within that relationship, i.e. how much learning comes from the experience itself and how much comes from the communication of ideas, feelings, shared perceptions.

F. Efficient teaching and learning involves an awareness of the overall context of learning.

The context can be the learner himself, i.e. the whole child cliché. It can refer to the learning environment, i.e. the physical, social, cultural, political, etc.

It can also refer to the relationships within the curricula, i.e. between subject areas.

Correlation of constructs. Andrew's comments on the pairs of constructs with high correltions were as follows:

Constructs C4 and C5
An awareness of the overall content of learning involves:

the language used
the teaching styles
the learning styles
individual rates of development
learning content
physical environment

Constructs C9 and C10
The key concepts are relevance and interaction: relevance requires interaction, and interaction requires relevance.

Constructs C3 and C4
Appropriate teaching methods and styles involve:

awareness of discovery approaches
awareness of language
awareness of individual learning rates

Constructs C1 and C3
Personally relevant learning experiences relate very closely to discovery approaches. Given experiences rely very heavily on language to create relevance.

Constructs C1 and C4
Personally relevant experiences are created by matching teaching styles to individual development.

Constructs C5 and C8
I cannot think of a reason for this high correlation!

Constructs C7 and C8
Significant learning experiences are provided by a balanced learning approach.

General interpretation. As argued previously, elements H, I and J may be removed from the grid. An inspection of the grid suggested reversing the poles of constructs C6, C7, C9 and C10. If this is done, the grid is as shown in Table 6.45.

The correlation matrix for the elements remains unaltered by any reversal of construct poles. The correlation matrix for the construct is as shown in Table 6.46. The median construct correlation score is 4. Hence the adjusted correlation matrix is as in Table 6.47.

With the reversal of the poles of constructs C6, C7, C9 and C10 there is no effective change in the plausibility of the constructs.

Table 6.45. Revised Repertory Grid

Construct	Elements							Construct
Initial pole	A	B	C	D	E	F	G	Emergent pole
C1P1	√	X	√	X	X	√	X	C1P2
C2P1	√	X	√	√	X	X	√	C2P2
C3P1	√	X	√	X	√	√	X	C3P2
C4P1	√	X	√	X	√	√	X	C4P2
C5P1	√	√	√	X	√	√	X	C5P2
C6P2	√	√	√	√	√	√	X	C6P1
C7P2	√	X	√	X	X	√	X	C7P1
C8P1	√	√	√	√	X	X	√	C8P2
C9P2	√	√	√	√	√	√	X	C9P1
C10P2	√	√	√	√	X	√	√	C10P2

Table 6.46. Correlation Matrix for Constructs

Construct	C1	C2	C3	C4	C5	C6	C7	C8	C9	C10
C1		4	6	6	5	4	7	3	4	4
C2			3	3	2	3	4	6	3	5
C3				7	6	5	6	2	5	3
C4					6	5	6	2	5	3
C5						6	5	3	6	4
C6							4	4	7	5
C7								3	4	4
C8									4	6
C9										5
C10										

Table 6.47. Adjusted Correlation Matrix for Constructs

Construct	C1	C2	C3	C4	C5	C6	C7	C8	C9	C10
C1		0	2	2	1	0	3	0	0	0
C2			0	0	1	0	0	2	0	1
C3				3	2	1	2	1	1	0
C4					2	1	2	1	1	0
C5						2	1	0	2	0
C6							0	0	3	1
C7								0	0	0
C8									0	2
C9										1
C10										

Repertory Grid 3

This grid was completed by Andrew at the end of the teacher development program.

Elements of the Grid

These were as follows:

Element	Statement of element
A	Effective learning involves a high degree of interacting between the teacher and the students.
B	Effective learning involves the developing of children's general abilities.
C	Effective learning involves significant experiences that have intrinsic value.
D	Effective learning involves a supportive environment.
E	Effective learning involves recognizing individuals.
F	Effective learning involves communicating understandings.
G	Effective learning involves a sense of purpose.

H   Effictive learning involves various ways of experiencing.
I   Effective learning is dynamic.

Constructs

Using the triad method described in Chapter 2, the following bipolar constructs were elicited:

Construct	Initial pole	Emergent pole
C1	Interaction between teachers and students involves significant experiences of intrinsic values.	The development of children's abilities involves significant experiences of intrinsic values.
C2	A supportive environment develops children's general abilities.	A supportive environment involves significant experiences that have intrinsic value.
C3	A supportive environment involves recognizing individuals.	Significant experiences of intrinsic worth involve recognizing individuals.
C4	Communicating understanding involves a supportive environment.	Communicating understanding involves recognizing individuals.
C5	A sense of purpose involves communicating understandings.	A sense of purpose involves recognizing individuals.
C6	Communicating understandings involves various ways of teaching.	Communicating understandings involves a sense of purpose.
C7	A sense of purpose is dynamic.	Various ways of experience are dynamic.
C8	A supportive environment involves a high degree of interaction.	A supportive environment involves a sense of purpose.
C9	Developing general abilities involves recognizing individuals.	Developing general abilities involves various ways of experiencing.
C10	Significant experiences of intrinsic value are dynamic.	Significant experiences of intrinsic value involve communicating understandings.

Table 6.48.   Repertory Grid 3

Constructs	Elements									Constructs
Initial pole	A	B	C	D	E	F	G	H	I	Emergent pole
C1P1	√	X	√	√	√	√	√	√	√	C1P2
C2P1	X	√	X	X	X	√	√	X	X	C2P2
C3P1	√	√	X	√	X	√	√	X	√	C3P2
C4P1	X	X	X	√	X	X	X	X	X	C4P2
C5P1	√	X	X	√	X	√	√	X	X	C5P2
C6P1	√	X	√	X	√	X	X	√	√	C6P2
C7P1	√	√	X	√	X	√	√	X	√	C7P2
C8P1	√	X	√	√	√	X	X	√	√	C8P2
C9P1	√	√	√	√	√	√	√	X	√	C9P2
C10P1	√	X	√	X	√	X	X	√	√	C10P2

Repertory Grid

Andrew then completed the repertory grid as shown in Table 6.48.

Correlation Matrices

These correlation matrices were then completed and are shown in Tables 6.49 and 6.50.

Coefficients of Consistency and Plausibility

These were 0.57 and 0.28 respectively.

The median construct scores for the range of 0 to 9 are 4 and 5. Therefore, the adjusted construct correlation matrix is as shown in Table 6.51.

Table 6.49. Correlation Matrix for Elements

Element	A	B	C	D	E	F	G	H	I
A		4	7	7	7	6	6	6	9
B			3	5	3	8	8	2	5
C				4	10	3	3	9	8
D					4	7	7	3	6
E						3	3	9	8
F							10	2	5
G								2	5
H									7
I									

Table 6.50. Correlation Matrix for Constructs

Construct	1	2	3	4	5	6	7	8	9	10
1		2	5	2	5	6	5	7	7	6
2			6	5	6	1	6	0	4	1
3				4	7	2	9	3	7	2
4					6	3	4	4	2	3
5						2	7	3	5	2
6							2	8	4	9
7								3	6	2
8									5	8
9										4
10										

Evaluation of the Effectiveness of the Touchstone Approach

Table 6.51. Adjusted Correlation Matrix for Constructs

Construct	1	2	3	4	5	6	7	8	9	10
1		2	0	2	0	1	0	2	2	1
2			1	0	1	3	1	4	0	3
3				0	2	2	4	1	2	2
4					1	1	0	0	2	1
5						2	2	1	0	2
6							2	3	0	4
7								1	1	2
8									0	3
9										0
10										

Interpretation of the Repertory Grid and Correlation Matrices

Co-referencing of elements. The elements and their referents are as follows:

Element	R1	R2	R3
A	Interacting	Teachers	Students
B	Development	Children's abilities	
C	Significant experience	Intrinsic values	
D	Supportive environment		
E	Recognizing	Involved	
F	Communicating	Understandings	
G	Sense of purpose		
H	Experiences		
I	Dynamism		

As can be seen from the table, there is very little co-referencing between elements.

Highly correlated pairs of elements. Andrew's comments on these were as follows:

Elements A and I (9/10)
The dynamic nature of learning is a result of interactions.

Elements E and H, and C and H (9/10 and 9/10)
Each individual has a preferred learning style.

Elements C and E (10/10)
The needs and interests of individuals need to be taken into consideration so that learning experiences will be meaningful.

Elements F and G (10/10)
The purpose of learning is to enable some common agreements or understandings to be reached.

This correlation helps me the most in coming to terms with the conflict I have sometimes felt between meeting the needs of individuals and the needs of myself as a teacher. For me, it means finding some common ground, whereby both learners and teacher can satisfy their individual needs.

In my focus class, the search for this common ground is the basis for my operation (as a teacher).

Pairs of elements with low correlations. Andrew's comments on these were as follows:

Elements B and H (2/10)
The low correlation perhaps indicates some confusion over the best possible ways for developing children's abilities. Certainly, for my focus a variety of experiences is provided.

Elements G and H and F and H (2/10 and 2/10)
The low correlations indicate not confusion as first thought, but reinforcement of the fact that a variety of experiences is necessary. The low correlaton indicates that different experiences are relevant in different circumstances.

He went on to say that:

Having examined the grid closely, the following issues appear to emerge. I equate supportive environment with

(a)   recognizing intrinsic value;

(b)   common understanding, and

(c)   interaction.

For the focus class this indicates a highly personal teaching approach.

(b)   Various ways of experiencing allow for individual learning styles. There is a general assumption that 'first hand experiences' are best. It may be that it is not the type of experience that counts but how well that experience fits the needs of the individual.

My focus class is an unusual collection. Certainly experiences that are normally successful for other children are not always successful in this group.

(c)   There is a conflict of interest, at times, between group needs and individual needs.

For my focus class, I am more aware of the need to develop group cohesiveness and identity because of the egocentric nature of the children.

Perhaps this indicates that a highly individual approach to learning is fine if the children already possess group skills. If they do not then the development of empathy for others is vital.

(d)   The development of general abilities provides me with a sense of pupose.

The focus class lacks the ability to see relationships, connections, between learning experiences. My role is to develop their insights into relationships. Thus the teaching program is not a lock-step, sequenced approach aimed at developing specific subskills. This latter approach is often the approach taken when teaching 'remedial readers'.

Changes in Consistency and Plausibility throughout the Program

For Andrew, the coefficients of consistency and plausibility for the three repertory grids were as follows:

	Repertory Grid		
Coefficient of	1	2	3
Consistency	0.77	0.55	0.57
Plausibility	0.49	0.30	0.28

The increasing awareness of alternative perspectives of teaching and learning facilitated by the teacher development program, and the conflicts Andrew has described in relation to his role in providing effective teaching and learning for the focus class, have made it difficult for him to give a highly consistent and plausible description of effective teaching and learning for that class. This conflict is also indicated by Andrew's apparent inability to give a plausible interpretation of the reasonably consistent descriptions he was giving.

The repertory grid procedures for monitoring consistency, co-reference and plausibility have helped Andrew identify his strongly held beliefs about effective teaching and learning, and the clash between these and his perception of the needs of the students in the focus class. Providing a more intelligible, coherent and plausible description of effective teaching and learning for this class will entail the resolution of this conflict.

Evaluation of the Effectiveness of the Program in Meeting Its General Purposes

The three case studies described in this chapter have included participants' interpretations and analyses of the three repertory grids they developed during the teacher development program. For each of these repertory grids, in each case study:

   i   the elements describing effective teaching and learning for the focus class, the constructs elicited from these elements and the repertory grid formed by these elements and constructs were listed;

   ii   correlation matrices for both elements and constructs were completed;

   iii   the coefficients of consistency and plausibility were computed;

   iv   an interpretation of the repertory grid, its correlation matrices and the coefficients of consistency and plausibility was undertaken.

For each set of three repertory grids, for each of the three cases considered, the changes in the coefficients of consistency and plausibility and the teachers' interpretations of these changes were discussed. All of the above were then used to discuss the changes, if any, in the intelligibility of the descriptions of effective teaching and learning given by the teachers.

In case A the initial descriptions given for effective teaching and learning had coefficients of consistency and plausibility of 0.83 and 0.71 respectively. These were reduced to 0.59 and 0.24 respectively for Repertory Grid 2. This reduction was seen to result from an increased awareness by teacher A of a greater range of possible alternative descriptions for effective teaching and learning. At the same time an analysis of this grid indicated the retention of some 'core factors' by the teacher in describing effective teaching and learning. Repertory Grid 3 used a wider range of referents in its elements, and had higher coefficients of consistency and plausibility of 0.84 and 0.86 respectively. This was interpreted to indicate that the teacher had been able to accommodate a wider range of educational perspectives in the description of effective teaching and learning.

The changes in the coefficients during the program indicate that the consistency of the descriptions of effective teaching and learning has been retained at a high level, and that there was a significant increase in the plausibility of this description, 0.71 to 0.86, or 0.76 to 1.0 for the adjusted repertory grid. This appears to indicate that participation in the program has not changed the logical consistency of the description given, but has increased the teacher's capacity to give plausible interpretations of these descriptions. That is, a core of elements has been retained by the teacher, but these elements may now be given more plausible interpretations. In this sense the intelligibility of the descriptions of effective teaching and learning given by this teacher has been enhanced.

For teacher B, each set of elements produced for the three repertory grids contained a core set of elements. As the program progressed, this core became more clearly focused on the participant's role as a teacher, and on the practical constraints on her position. The conflict between these two factors was highlighted, but not resolved, by the program. This lack of resolution agrees with the lack of any significant change in the coefficients of consistency and plausibility throughout the program. This participant will not be able to give a more consistent and plausible, and hence more intelligible, description of effective teaching and learning until this conflict is resolved or removed.

In a similar way, for teacher C

The increasing awareness of alternative perspectives of teaching and learning facilitated by the teacher development program, and the conflicts the teacher has described in relation to his role in providing effective teaching and learning for the focus class, have made it difficult for the teacher to give a highly consistent and plausible description of effective teaching and learning for that class. For this case, the repertory grid procedures for monitoring consistency, co-referencing and plausibility have helped this teacher identify his strongly held beliefs about effective teaching and learning, and the clash between these and his perception of the needs of his students in the focus class. Providing a more intelligible, coherent and plausible description of effective teaching and learning will entail the resolution of this conflict.

For teacher A, descriptive intelligibility for effective teaching and learning has been enhanced. For teachers B and C, an increase in descriptive intelligibility depends upon the solution of a conflict relating to their perceptions of teaching and learning. That is, whilst descriptive intelligibility has not been enhanced for teachers B and C, a condition necessary for this enhancement has been clearly identified. This condition may be made a focus for any further teacher development.

In all three cases the procedures developed for analyzing and interpreting repertory grids for descriptions of effective teaching and learning have been applied successfully to monitoring changes in the co-referencing, consistency and plausibility of these descriptions. To the extent that co-referencing, consistency and plausibility are contributing factors to intelligibility, these procedures have permitted the monitoring and assessing of changes in the intelligibility of these descriptions of effective teaching and learning.

Chapter 7

Applications of the Touchstone Approach to Teacher Development

The Touchstone Approach

The touchstone approach to teacher development may be summarized in terms of:

> the purposes of the teacher development program, including individual teacher purposes, group purposes and the general purposes of the program;

> the theoretical assumptions underpinning the program, including the assumption of a coherentist epistemology, a touchstone approach to theory development and Kelly's (1955) theory of personal constructs;

> the problem to be studied during the program, such as describing effective teaching and learning;

> the problems of planning, conducting and evaluating the effectiveness of the teacher development program, and of monitoring and assessing the changes in intelligibility of the descriptions given as possible solutions to the problem being studied.

This approach, as illustrated in the previous chapters, can be used as a general approach to the planning, conduct and evaluation of teacher development programs. Teacher development is seen as enhancing the intelligibility of the descriptions teachers give as possible solutions to the problem being studied in the teacher development program. Enhanced intelligibility is indicated by an increase in the co-referencing, consistency and practical plausibility of the descriptions given by the teachers.

If the interaction of teacher, curriculum and organizational development is assumed, a problem in any of these areas can be investigated in terms of the influence of the changes in one or both of the other two areas on the problem. Thus a problem in teaching and learning can be investigated by considering the influence of changes in the curriculum and/or the organization sponsoring the curriculum and its teaching. An organizational problem, such as effective decision-making in a school, can be studied in terms of the influence changes in the curriculum of that school have on it. In this case the problem was describing effective teaching and learning, and this was studied by considering the influence of changes in the approach to curriculum development on it.

Suppose A denotes an activity in an educational organization, which is directed towards meeting the purposes of that organization. Of central interest to those within the organization, who are associated with that activity, is its effectiveness in meeting its stated purposes. Thus the interest in a school in activities such as teaching and learning, decision-making and student counselling, for example, is in the effectiveness of each of these activities in meeting school purposes. Such activities are linked with teacher development, curriculum development and organizational development.

Given the interaction of these aspects of any educational organization, the problem of describing effective A (decision-making, teaching, learning, student counselling, budget policy development, etc.) can be studied in a similar way to that used for the problem of describing effective teaching and learning: that is, by using a teacher development program focused on the problem of describing effective A.

In this case, the purposes of the teacher development program are, as described earlier, as follows:

1   *Individual teacher purposes*
    These purposes are to enhance each participant's capacities to describe, intelligibly, effective A by developing their capacities to:
    i   recognize and describe;
    ii   explore;
    iii review;
    iv   revise and clarify alternative frames of reference which they may use to describe effective A.
2   *Group purposes*
    These purposes are to enhance each participant's capacities to describe, intelligibly, effective A by developing their capacities to:

     i   communicate;
     ii share;
     iii negotiate these frames of reference with other program participants.

3 *General purposes*

The general purposes are:

     i   to monitor and assess changes in the intelligibility of each participant's descriptions of effective teaching and learning throughout the teacher development program;
     ii to enhance the intelligibility of each participant's descriptions of effective teaching and learning though participation in the teacher development program.

Thus the problem of describing effective A can be studied using a teacher development program similar to that described in this study, using the same procedures to:

1 plan and conduct the program;
2 develop the reading content for the program;
3 monitor and assess the changes in intelligibility of the participants' descriptions of effective A;
4 evaluate the program.

That is, the procedures developed for the planning, conduct and evaluation of this teacher development program can be used as a general approach to planning, conducting and evaluating teacher development programs provided that the purposes for participants in the program are as given in the 'Introduction' and the problem to be investigated by the participants is of the form 'describing effective A', where A is a purposeful phenomenon of an educational organization. In using this approach

     i   the modifications suggested above would need to be considered; and
     ii the intelligibility of the participants' descriptions of effective A can be monitored and assessed in terms of their co-referencing, consistency and plausibility, but will not necessarily be enhanced. The procedures embodied within this approach do, however, facilitate the systematic study of factors influencing this intelligibility, and hence provide a basis for designing further programs for its enhancement.

Applications of the Touchstone Approach

The touchstone approach to teacher development is applicable to the study of a wide range of problems, including the problem of describing the effectiveness of any phenomenon occurring within a school. Such phenomena could include decision-making, teaching, learning, consulting, coaching, assessing, leading, sharing, reviewing and negotiating. A brief discussion of some possible applications follows.

Collegial Decision-making

Given current emphases in education on collegial participation in decision-making, and the processes, such as cooperating, sharing and negotiating which are associated with it, the touchstone approach can be applied to descriptions of any of the phases of this decision-making. In this way the effectiveness of each phase, and hence of the total process, could be evaluated. Such evaluations would form the basis for modifying the processes being used and thus making them more effective.

Parent Participation

Recently, there has been an increased emphasis on parents participating in the decision-making of their schools. While schools may be strongly committed to having parents more directly involved in the life of the schools, questions will arise as to the effectiveness of this participation, and, in particular, whether such participation is educationally effective. Focusing on the problem of describing educationally effective participation, a program, possibly involving both teachers and parents for a particular school, could be developed, conducted and evaluated using the touchstone approach. This would enable both the monitoring and evaluation of the educational effectiveness of the participation.

Negotiating the Curriculum

Much recent literature on curriculum development has proposed student negotiation as a central concept in this development. However, it may not always be clear what is to be understood as negotiating and under what circumstances the negotiation is effective. Describing effective negotiation can be studied using the touchstone approach, and through this study more effective ways of negotiation found.

Critically Reflecting on Teaching

As the demands for school accountability increase, and schools come under increasing public scrutiny, teachers are being required to be more publicly accountable in terms of both the curriculum they teach and the ways in which they teach.

At the heart of the debate concerning teacher accountability is the conflict between seeing the teacher as a skilled technician and as a critically reflective practitioner. Those who support critical reflection, and the accompanying self-appraisal, as crucial to teacher development will be faced with understanding and describing publicly what is meant by critically reflecting. The touchstone approach can be used to study, and enhance the intelligibility of, descriptions of critically reflecting. As for all phenomena studied, it is likely that the study will lead to perceiving the phenomena in terms of a series of contributing processes. Thus the process of reflection could be seen to involve describing, sharing, negotiating, reviewing and revising. These processes, or substages, become important in planning programs so that each stage is recognized and is carefully related to the other stages.

Implementing Changes

Much has been written on implementing change, but the implementation phase of most projects is often its most difficult and problematic stage. The touchstone approach would enable the processes involved in implementation in relation to a particular project to be studied, monitored and evaluated. In this way increasingly intelligible descriptions of implementing could be developed leading to an enhanced understanding of this phenomenon.

Teaching

As illustrated by the three case studies described earlier, the touchstone approach can be used to study the effectiveness of teaching. In particular, it can be used as the basis for a teacher to monitor and critically reflect on practice. As self-appraisal is now seen as central to improving the effectiveness of teaching, having teachers participate in a teacher development program using the touchstone approach is an excellent way of promoting self-appraisal.

Whatever process is being studied for its effectiveness, the touch-

stone approach can be used to monitor the enhancement of this effectiveness as it occurs, and to evaluate the effectiveness of the teacher
development program being used. Descriptions of the process being
studied will be the focus of the teacher development program, and
enhancing the intelligibility of these descriptions the major purpose of the
program. Through such programs there will be an overall enhancement of
the intelligibility of the general educational discourse.

The intelligibility of this discourse is *a* crucial, if not *the* crucial,
factor in helping all parties who have a stake in education to become
intelligent participants in this discourse; thus it provides a basis for public
accountability. Application of the touchstone approach to the study of
selected phenomena in schools through teacher development programs is
important in developing the public accountability of schools and their
teachers.

Recommendations for Applying the Touchstone Approach

The teachers who participated in the trialling of the touchstone approach
identified several factors as being very important when applying this
approach. These were the need to:

  i   include activities to help participants become familiar with the
      procedures for developing and interpreting repertory grids early
      in the program;
  ii ensure that the reading and lecture input made by those conduct-
      ing the program are significantly related to the problem being
      studied, and, in particular, that the language and terms used are
      easily intelligible to participants;
  iii include strategies for sustaining the motivation and involvement
      of the participants during the entire period of the program;
  iv make sure that each participant is frequently made aware of
      progress throughout the program.

Developing and Interpreting Repertory Grids

This is likely to be the most difficult aspect of the approach with which
participants need to become comfortable and competent. To a large
degree this is due to the unfamiliar procedures and ways of thinking
involved. Personal construct theory is not usually taught in either pre-
service or postgraduate courses in teacher education. As well, the capacity

of construct theory to inquire into the personal values and beliefs of teachers is considerable. Such inquiries, particularly as they are to some extent made public by the participants needing to share insights, may be initially, and for some may remain, personally threatening.

The anxiety experienced by participants may be compounded by difficulties in becoming competent in constructing the repertory grids. In particular, problems may arise as participants begin to elicit constructs from their sets of elements. This, in part, is likely to be due to them not being used to considering what may be presupposed by the elements they have chosen, and what is the touchstone between the different sets of presuppositions of these elements.

Those conducting the program should be prepared to proceed very carefully and slowly when introducing the development interpretation of repertory grids. A range of activities, such as those suggested earlier and as found in the literature on repertory grids, should be used for this introduction, and care should be taken at all stages to discuss any difficulties experienced by the participants. The case studies described earlier may be used to illustrate the potential of the approach to provide significant insights into the problem being studied.

Intelligibility of Program Readings

As indicated earlier, the readings chosen should be such that they connect easily and significantly with the problem being studied. If, for example, the problem being studied is parent participation in school decision-making, the readings chosen as input to the program should provide the participants with new and insightful ways of thinking about this participation. Literature relating to models of decision-making in organizations could serve such a purpose. It may be necessary to begin by helping participants explore the ways of thinking, or constructs, being used in the literature, and to use this exploration to develop bipolar constructs. These constructs may then be applied to the elements which have been developed to describe the problem. The approaches described earlier in this book will be helpful in this regard.

Much of the literature which could be used as reading input may require some modification. In particular, participants may have difficulties if unfamiliar terms are used without some prior discussion and consideration. This has important implications for the enhancement of the intelligibility of the discourse the participants develop in relation to the problem being studied. If the readings remain unintelligible, so will the participants' discourse developed during the program.

Sustaining Motivation and Indicating Progress

Sustaining participant motivation throughout the program will depend largely on the extent to which participants become comfortable and competent in the development and interpretation of repertory grids. Whilst relevant strategies have been discussed previously, there will be an additional need for frequent one-to-one discussions with each participant. As well as providing assistance in developing and interpreting the repertory grids, these discussions should give support to the participant and a clear indication of the progress being made. Within these discussions it will be important to help each participant come to see their personal theories of teaching and how these impinge on their practice. One way of providing additional feedback is the inclusion of regular tutorial sessions. By seeing more clearly the interaction between teacher action and teacher theories of teaching, the participants' appreciation of the touchstone approach will be enhanced.

Conclusion

The touchstone approach to theory development, as described and illustrated in this book, gives a theoretical and practical basis for:

   i   planning and conducting a teacher development program;
  ii developing the reading input for this program;
 iii monitoring and assessing the changes in the intelligibility of the participants' descriptions of effective educational phenomena;
 iv evaluating the effectiveness of this teacher development program.

For this approach, teacher development is seen as the enhancement of the intelligibility of these descriptions of educational phenomena. Teacher development programs based on the touchstone approach lead towards an increasingly intelligible, and publicly accountable, educational discourse.

Bibliography

(Works used in developing the reading units for the program are included.)

ALLEN, R. (1978) 'The Philosophy of Michael Polanyi, and Its Significance for Education', *Journal of Philosophy of Education*, 12, 167–77.

ARCHAMBAULT, R. (1965) *Philosophical Analysis and Education*. London: Routledge and Kegan Paul.

BANNISTER, D. (1970) *Perspective on Personal Construct Theory*. London: Academic Press.

BANNISTER, D. (1977) *New Perspectives in Personal Construct Theory*. London: Academic Press.

BANNISTER, D. and FRANSELLA, F. (1971) *Inquiring Man: The Theory of Personal Constructs*. London: Penguin.

BANNISTER, D. and FRANSELLA, F. (1977) *A Manual for Repertory Grid Technique*. London: Academic Press.

BANNISTER, D. and FRANSELLA, F. (1978) *Personal Construct Psychology*. London: Academic Press.

BANNISTER, D. and FRANSELLA, F. (1982) *Inquiring Man: The Psychology of Personal Constructs*. Harmondsworth: Penguin.

BANNISTER, D. and MOIR, J. (1968) *The Evaluation of Personal Constructs*. London: Academic Press.

BANNISTER, D. and SALMON, P. (1975) 'A Personal Construct View of Education', *Universal Education Quarterly*, 6, 28–31.

BANTOCK, C. (1980) *Studies in the History of Educational Theory*. London: George Allen and Unwin.

BEARD, R. (1977) 'Teachers' and Pupils' Construing of Reading'. Paper presented at the Second International Congress on Personal Construct Theory, Christchurch College, Oxford.

BIERI, J. (1966) *Clinical and Social Judgement: The Discrimination of Behavioural Information*. New York: John Wiley.

BENJAFIELD, J. and ADAMS-WEBBER, J. (1975) 'Assimilative Projection and Construct Balance in the Repertory Grid', *British Journal of Psychology*, 66, 2, 169–73.

BEN-PERETZ, M., *et al.* (1986) *Advances on Research on Teacher Thinking*. Lisse: Swets and Zeitlinger.

BERLAK, A. and BERLAK, H. (1981) *Dilemmas of Schooling: Teaching and Social Change*. London: Methuen.

BLOOM, B., *et al.* (1956) *Taxonomy of Educational Objectives, Book 1: Cognitive Domain*. New York: Longmans.

BOLTON, N. (1979) 'Phenomenology and Education', *British Journal of Educational Studies*, 27, 3, 245–58.

BONARIUS, J. (1965) 'Research in the Personal Construct Theory of George A. Kelly: Role Construct Repertory Test and Basic Theory', in B. MAHER (Ed.), *Progress in Experimental Personality Research*, 2, 2–46, New York: Academic Press.

BONARIUS, H., HOLLAND, R. and ROSENBERG, S. (Eds) (1981) *Personal Construct Psychology: Recent Advances in Its Theory and Practice*. London: Macmillan.

BONJOUR, L. (1985) *The Structure of Empirical Knowledge*. Cambridge, Mass: Harvard University Press.

BRENT, A. (1978) *Philosopical Foundations for the Curriculum*. London: George Allen and Unwin.

BROOK, J. (1979) 'A Repertory Grid Analysis of Perceptions of Counselling Roles', *Journal of Vocational Behaviour* 15, 1, 25–35.

BROWN, S. (Ed.) (1975) *Philosophers Discuss Education*. London: Macmillan.

BUCHMANN, M. (1984) 'The Use of Research Knowledge in Teaching and Teacher Education', *American Journal of Education*, 9, 4, 421–39.

CLARK, C. (1986) 'Ten Years of Conceptual Development in Research on Teacher Thinking', in M. BEN-PERETZ *et al.*, *Advances on Research on Teacher Thinking*. Lisse: Swets and Zeitlinger.

CLANDININ, D. (1985) 'Personal Practical Knowledge: A Study of Teachers' Classroom Images', *Curriculum Inquiry*, 15, 4, 361–5.

CLANDININ, D. JEAN and CONNELLY, F. MICHAEL (1986) 'What Is "Personal" in Studies of the Personal', in M. BEN-PERETZ *et al.*, *Advances on Research on Teacher Thinking*. Lisse: Swets and Zeitlinger.

COPE (1972) *Committee on Primary Education*. Hobart: Education Department of Tasmania.

CROMWELL, R. and CALDWELL, D. (1962) 'A Comparison of Ratings

Based on Personal Constructs of Self and Others', *Journal of Clinical Psychology*, 18, 43–6.

DEARDEN, R. (1980) 'What Is General about General Education?', *Oxford Review of Education*, 6, 3, 279–88.

DEWEY, J. (1916) *Democracy and Education*. New York: Macmillan.

DUCK, S. (1973) *Personal Relationships and Personal Constructs: A Study of Friendship Information*. New York: John Wiley.

DUCKWORTH, D. and ENTWISTLE, N. (1974) 'Attitudes to School Subjects: A Repertory Grid Technique', *British Journal of Educational Psychology*, 44, 1, 76–83.

ELBAZ, F. (1983) *Teacher Thinking: A Study of Practical Knowledge*. New York: Nichols.

ELLIOTT, J. (1975) 'Education and Human Beings', in S. BROWN (Ed.), *Philosophers Discuss Education*. London: Macmillan.

ERICKSON, F. (1986) 'Qualitative Methods in Research on Teaching', in M. WITTROCK (Ed.), *Handbook of Research in Teaching*. 3rd ed. New York: Macmillan.

FAY, B. (1977) 'How People Change Themselves: The Relationship between Contract Theory and Its Audience', in T. BALL (Ed.), *Political Theory and Praxis: New Perspectives*. Minneapolis, Minn.: Minnesota Press.

FLODEN, R. (1983) 'Actively Learning to Be Expert: A New View of Learning'. Paper presented to the Annual Meeting of the American Association of Colleges of Teacher Education, Detroit.

GARDNER, P. (1979) 'Structure-of-knowledge Theory and Science Education', *Educational Philosophy and Theory*, 4, 2, 25–46.

GIBBONS, J. (1979) 'Curriculum Integration', *Curriculum Inquiry*, 9, 321–32.

GOWER, J. (1977) 'The Analysis of Three-way Grids', in P. SLATER (Ed.), *Dimensions of Intra-Personal Space*. Vol. 2. New York: John Wiley.

GREEN, T. (1971) *The Activities of Teaching*. New York: McGraw-Hill.

HALKES, R. and OLSEN, J. (Eds) (1984) 'Teacher Thinking: A New Perspective on Persisting Problems in Education', in *Proceedings of the First Symposium of the International Study Association of Teacher Thinking*, Tolburg, October, 1983. Lisse: Swets and Zeitlinger.

HAMLYN, D. (1978) *Experience and the Growth of Understanding*. London: Routledge and Kegan Paul.

HIRST, P. (1974) *Knowledge and the Curriculum*. London: Routledge and Kegan Paul.

HIRST, P. (1974) 'Liberal Education and the Nature of Knowledge', in P. HIRST, *Knowledge and the Curriculum*. London: Routledge and Kegan Paul.

HIRST, P. and PETERS, R. (1970) *The Logic of Education*. London: Routledge and Kegan Paul.

HONEY, P. (1979) Series of articles on using repertory grids, *Industrial and Commercial Training*, September–November 1979, John Wellans Publication.

HONIKMAN, B. (1976) 'Construct Theory as an Approach to Architectural and Environmental Design', in P. SLATER (Ed.), *Explorations of Interpersonal Space*, Vol. 1. London: John Wiley and Sons.

HOSPERS, J. (1973) *An Introduction to Philosophical Analysis*. Rev. ed. London: Routledge and Kegan Paul.

HOWE, M. (Ed.) (1977) *Adult Learning: Psychological Research and Applications*. New York: John Wiley.

HUME, D. (1962) *A Treatise on Human Nature*. Book 1. London: Collins Fontana Library.

JOHNSON-LAIRD, P. (1983) *Mental Models: Towards a Cognitive Science of Language, Inference and Consciousness*. Cambridge: Cambridge University Press.

KEEN, T.R. (1977) 'TARGET: Teaching Appraisal by Repertory Grid Techniques'. Paper presented at the Second International Congress on Personal Construct Theory, Christchurch College, Oxford.

KEEN, T.R. (1978) 'Repertory Grid Techniques for Teacher Appraisal', in *Staff Development in Higher Education*. Guilford: SRHE, 72–84.

KEEN, T.R. (1978) 'Developing Students' Learning Skills', *Teaching News*, 5, 19.

KEEN, T.R. (1979) 'Pedagogic Styles in Physics Education: An Attitude Scaling and Repertory Grid Study'. PhD thesis. Milton Keynes: Open University.

KELLY, A. (1982) *The Curriculum: Theory and Practice*. London: Harper and Row.

KELLY, G.A. (1955) *The Psychology of Personal Constructs*. Vols 1 and 2. New York: Norton.

KELLY, G.A. (1969) 'Clinical Psychology and Personality' in B. MAHER (Ed.), *The Selected Papers of George A. Kelly*. New York: John Wiley and Sons.

KERR, I. (1976) *John Henry Newman: The Idea of a University*. London: Oxford University Press.

KEVILL, F. and SHAW, M. (1980) 'A Repertory Grid Study of Staff-Student Interactions', *Psychology Teaching*, 8, 29–36.

KEVILL, F., SHAW, M. and GOODACRE, E. (1978) 'In-Service Diploma Course Evaluation Using Repertory Grids', *British Journal of Educational Research*, 8, 1, 28–37.

KORNER, S. (1969) *Fundamental Questions in Philosophy*. Harmondsworth: Penguin.

KUHN, T. (1970) *The Structure of Scientific Revolutions*. Chicago, Ill.: University of Chicago Press.

LAKATOFF, G. and JOHNSON, M. (1980) *Metaphors We Live By*. Chicago, Ill.: Chicago University Press.

LAKATOS, I. and MUSGRAVE, A. (Eds) (1970) *Criticism and the Growth of Knowledge*. Cambridge: Cambridge University Press.

LAMPERT, M. (1985) 'How Do Teachers Manage to Teach: Perspectives on Problems in Practice', *Harvard Educational Review*, 55, 2, 178–94.

LARKIN, J., *et al.* (1980) 'Models of Competence in Solving Physics Problems', *Cognitive Science*, 4, 4, 317–45.

LAWTON, D. (1975) *Culture, Class and the Curriculum*. London: Routledge and Kegan Paul.

LEINHARDT, G. (1983) 'Routines in Expert Maths' Teachers Thoughts and Actions'. Paper presented at the annual meeting of American Educational Research Association, Montreal.

LEINHARDT, G., *et al.* (1984) 'Introduction and Integration of Classroom Continues'. Paper presented at the annual meeting of the American Educational Research Association, New Orleans.

LOCKE, J. (1976) *An Essay Concerning Human Understanding*. New abridged ed. Ed. by J.W. YOLTEN. London: J.M. Dent and Sons.

MAGEE, G. (1973) *Popper*. London: Fontana Collins.

MAHER, B. (Ed.) (1969) *Clinical Psychology and Personality: The Selected Papers of George Kelly*. New York: John Wiley

MANEUSO, J. and ADAMS-WEBBER, J. (Eds) (1982) *The Construing Person*. New York: Praeger.

MORGAN, K. (1975) 'Socialisation, Social Models, and the Open Education Movement: Some Philosophical Consideration', in D. NYBERG (Ed.), *Philosophy of Open Education*. London: Routledge and Kegan Paul.

MUNBY, H. (1983) 'A Qualitative Study of Teachers' Beliefs and Principles'. Paper presented at the annual meeting of the American Educational Research Association, Montreal, Canada.

NAGEL, E. (1957) 'Determinism and Development', in D. HARRIS (Ed.), *The Concept of Development*. Minneapolis, Minn.: University of Minnesota Press.

NEWMAN, J. (1853) *The Idea of a University: Defined and Illustrated*. Oxford: Clarendon Press.

NYBERG, D. (Ed.) (1975) *The Philosophy of Open Education*. London: Routledge and Kegan Paul.

OLSEN, J. (1980) 'Teacher Constructs and Curriculum Change: Innovative Doctrines and Practical Dilemmas'. Paper presented to the American Educational Research Association, Boston, Massachusetts.

OLSEN, J. (1981) 'Teacher Influence in the Classroom', *Instructional Science*, 10, 3, 259–75.

OLSEN, J. (Ed.) (1982) *Innovation in the American Curriculum*. London: Croom Helm.

OLSEN, J. (1985) 'Information Technology and Teacher Routines: Learning from the Microcomputer'. Paper presented at the ISATT Conference, Tilburg University, Netherlands.

OLSEN, J. and REID, W. (1982) 'Studying Innovations in Science Teaching: The Use of Repertory Grid Techniques in Developing a Research Strategy', *European Journal of Science Education*, 4, 2, 193–201.

PHENIX, P. (1964) *Realms of Meaning*. New York: McGraw-Hill.

PHILLIPS, E. (1980) 'Education for Research: The Changing Constructs of the Post-Graduate', *International Journal of Machine Studies* 13, 1, 39–48.

PITKIN, H. (1967) *The Concept of Representation*. Berkeley, Calif.: University of California Press.

POLANYI, M. (1958) *Study of Man*. London: Routledge and Kegan Paul.

POPE, M. (1977) 'Monitoring and Reflecting in Teacher Training: A Personal Construct Theory Approach'. Paper presented at the Second International Congress on Personal Construct Theory, Christchurch College, Oxford.

POPE, M. and KEEN, T. (1981) *Personal Construct Psychology and Education*. London: Academic Press.

POPE, M. and SCOTT, E. (1984) 'Teachers' Epistemology and Practice', in R. HALKES and J. OLSEN (Eds), *Teacher Thinking: A New Perspective on Persisting Problems in Education*. Lisse: Swets and Zeitlinger.

POPE, M. and SHAW, M. (1981) 'Negotiation in Learning', in H. BONARIUS *et al.* (Eds) *Personal Construct Psychology*. London: Macmillan Press.

POPE, M. and SHAW, M. (1981) 'Personal Construct Psychology in Education and Learning', *International Journal of Man-Machine Studies*, 14, 2, 223–32.

POPPER, K. (1963) *Conjectures and Refutations: The Growth of Scientific Knowledge*. London: Routledge and Kegan Paul.

REID, L. (1980) 'Literature and the Fine Arts as a Unique Form of Knowledge', *Cambridge Journal of Education*, 4, 3, 81–92.

RICHARDSON, F. and WEIGEL, R. (1969) 'Personal Construct Theory

Applied to the Marriage Relationship', in M. POPE and T. KEEN (1981), *Personal Construct Psychology and Education*. London: Academic Press.

ROTHBLATT, S. (1976) *Tradition and Change in English Liberal Education: An Essay in Culture and History*. London: Faber and Faber.

RORTY, R. (1980) *Philosophy and the Mirror of Nature*. Oxford: Basil Blackwell.

RYLE, G. (1949) *The Concept of Mind*. London: Hutchinson Press.

SCHÖN, D. (1983) *The Reflective Practitioner: How Professionals Think in Action*. New York: Basic Books.

SCHWAB, J. (1969) *College Curriculum and Student Protest*. Chicago, Ill.: University of Chicago Press.

SHAW, M. (1980) *On Becoming a Personal Scientist*. London: Academic Press.

SHAW, M. and GAINES, B. (1982) 'Tracking the Creativity Cycle with a Micro Computer', *International Journal of Man-Machine Studies*, 17, 1, 73–85.

SHAW, M. and THOMAS, L. (1978) 'Focus on Education: An Interactive Computer System for the Development and Analysis of Repertory Grids', *International Journal of Man-Machine Studies*, 10, 2, 139–73.

SHULMAN, L. and CAREY, N. (1975) 'Psychology and the Limitations of Individual Rationality: Implications for the Study of Reasoning and Civility', *Review of Educational Research*, 54, 501–24.

SMITH, M., HARTLEY, J. and STEWART, B. (1978) 'A Case of Repertory Grids Used in Vocational Guidance', *Journal of Occupational Psychology*, 51, 1, 97–104.

SMITH, R. (1981) 'Hirst's Unruly Theory: Forms of Knowledge, Truth and Meaning', *Educational Studies*, 7, 1, 17–26.

SMYTH, J. (1987) *Educating Teachers: Changing the Nature of Pedagogical Knowledge*. Lewes: Falmer Press.

SOLTIS, J. (1979) 'Knowledge and the Curriculum: A Review', *Teacher's College Record*, 80, 4, 771–84.

TABA, H. (1962) *Curriculum Development: Theory and Practice*. New York: Harcourt Brace Jovanovich.

THOMAS, L. and HARRIS-AUGSTEIN, E. (1977) 'Learning to Learn the Personal Construction of Meaning', in M. HOWE (Ed.), *Adult Learning: Psychological Research and Applications*. New York: John Wiley.

THOMAS, L. and HARRI-AUGSTEIN, S. (1985) *Self-organised Learning: Foundations of a Conversational Science of Psychology*. London: Routledge and Kegan Paul.

TIBERIUS, R. (1986) 'Metaphors Underlying the Improvement of Teaching', *British Journal of Technology*, 17, 2, 144–56.

TOM, A. (1984) *Teaching as a Moral Craft*. New York: Longman.

TULLY, J. (1976) 'Personal Construct Theory and Psychological Changes Related to Social Work Training', *British Journal of Social Work*, 6, 4, 481–9.

TYLER, R. (1950) *Basic Principles of Curriculum Development*. Chicago, Ill: University of Chicago Press.

WALKER, J. and EVERS, C. (1983) 'Professionalisation and Epistemic Privilege in the Politics of Educational Research', in *Educational Research for National Development: Policy, Planning and Politics*, Collected Papers, National Conference of the Australian Association for Research in Education, Australian National University, Canberra, November.

WALKER, J. and EVERS, C. (1984) 'Towards a Materialist Pragmatist Philosophy of Education', *Education Research and Perspectives*, 11, 1.

WALKLING, P. (1979) 'Structure of Knowledge Theory: A Refutation', *Educational Studies*, 5, 1, 61–72.

WEGENER, C. (1978) *Liberal Education and the Modern University*. Chicago, Ill.: University of Chicago Press.

WIDEEN, F. and ANDREWS, I. (1987) *Staff Development for School Improvement: A Focus on the Teacher*. Lewes: Falmer Press.

YAXLEY, B. (1987) 'Teacher Development as Enhancing Descriptive Intelligibility.' Unpublished PhD thesis, University of Tasmania.

YOUNG, M. (1971) *Knowledge and Control*. London: Collier-Macmillan.

Index